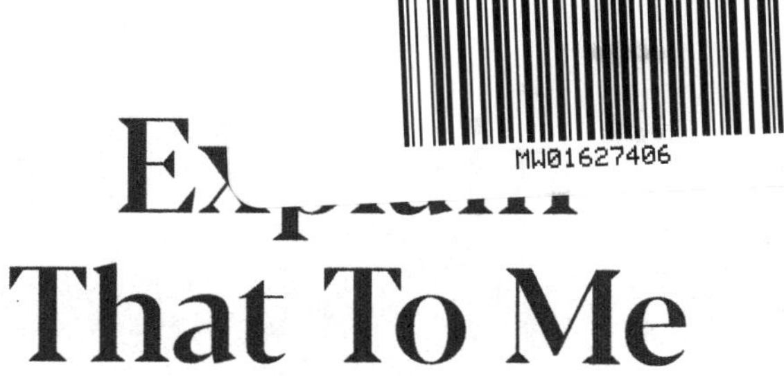

Explain That To Me

Signs & Symbols
of the
Catholic Church

Fr. John Noone

Explain That To Me,
Signs & Symbols of the Catholic Church

This book is published by Fr. John Noone.
It is reworked from the first edition in layout and in editing
by Carolyn Seal, OFS and Mary Lou Duncan, OFS
with addition of some drawings by Carolyn Seal, OFS.

Formatted for eBook and POD book by Booknook.biz.

Fr. John Noone's Books can be found on
https://frjohnnoonesbooks.wordpress.com/

ISBN 978-1-7351946-1-5

CONTENTS

INTRODUCTION

The Catholic Church is extremely rich in its teachings, symbols, traditions, customs, practices, etc. Some of these have roots in Old Testament times. Here is an attempt to explain in a short and simple way some of the more common symbols, customs, etc. that have developed in the Catholic Church over the past 2,000 years.

The word catholic is from the Greek word meaning universal and was used very early in the Church. St. Ignatius of Antioch (37-107 A.D.) used it in a letter to describe how the Church reaches out to all people everywhere. The term catholic was used in the Apostles Creed in the 2nd century. "I believe in the holy Catholic Church." In the Nicene Creed (4th century) the church is described as "One, Holy, Catholic and Apostolic."

PART ONE

SIGNS AND SYMBOLS – MATERIAL AND SPIRITUAL

Man is composed of body and soul, material and spiritual. We need some material things which can help us get to spiritual realities. The internal expression of the soul seeks to show itself in an external physical way, and the inner life is sustained by external acts. Human beings find it difficult to meditate on divine things. They need material things to help them, such as lights, incense, vestments, etc. People's minds are attracted to these material things which help them in their relationship with God.

People need signs and symbols to communicate with other people, such as language, gestures and actions. The same is true in relationship with God. Many signs, as the gestures of prayer (open arms, joined hands, kneeling, going in procession, etc.) are common to all people because we see these in different religious traditions.

Symbols are used in the world around us. The Catholic Church uses lots of symbols also.

A symbol is a visible sign of something that is invisible. It is an object that we can see which reminds us of something we cannot see. For instance, the lion is a symbol of courage, the cross is a symbol of Christianity. A Chinese proverb says, "One picture is worth a thousand words."

A symbol, or picture, is a short message. It is a visible sign of something spiritual that is real. Symbols are to be found among all people dating back thousands of years. The external sacrifices we offer to God are symbols or signs of the internal and true love of God and neighbor in our hearts.

Symbols are used plentifully in the Old and New Testaments. In the Old Testament in Genesis, the rainbow is a symbol of God's Covenant.

In the New Testament Jesus used symbols when He taught spiritual truths. The lost sheep is a symbol of the soul, which has been overcome by sin. Jesus calls Himself the vine in Jn 15:4-5; He calls Himself the door or gate for the sheep in Jn 10:7; and so on.

Art in the Church is mostly made up of symbols. There is a wealth of these symbols in the almost 374 miles or 600 kilometers of catacombs outside of the city of Rome. These underground passages, which average 7 or 8 feet high and 3 feet wide, are a treasure house of early Christian symbols. The catacombs were places where the early Christians buried their dead. From about 100 until about 400 A.D., the art of Christian symbols developed in these underground cemeteries. All of the symbols are to be understood in relationship to the teachings of the Catholic Church, the writings of the Fathers of the Church and the prayers of the Liturgy.

At first, the new Christians drew subjects from the Old Testament. The New Testament books were just written, but the Bible, as we know it today, was not yet compiled by the Catholic Church. That did not come about until about the year 400 A.D. Persecution was fierce at that time, so they used symbols to hide their identity and to teach the faith to those who came forward to commit themselves to Jesus Christ. Those early Christians used symbols that were familiar to all peoples, but those symbols were given a new meaning. Most of the Christian symbols we have today began on the walls of the catacombs in Rome.

Christianity became legal in 313 A.D. under the Emperor Constantine. From then on symbols of the faith did not have to be used to convey a secret message about the faith. However, over the next several hundred years symbols were drawn on pottery, glass, and mosaics.

Symbols were used in the churches to teach people about the faith since the people did not know how to read or write. Symbols are good in teaching the faith, but like everything else, cannot give us the full story. However, they can lift the mind from material things to truths which have been told to us by God.

SYMBOLS OF GOD

Triangle:

001

The Triangle is used as a symbol of God. No person has seen God, and no person can draw the Blessed Trinity or three persons in One God, the Father, the Son, and the Holy Spirit. However, a symbol of the Blessed Trinity is the equilateral triangle, which has 3 sides united and equal to each other. The Persons of the Blessed Trinity are equal to each other and united to each other. This is one of the oldest symbols for the Blessed Trinity.

Shamrock:

002

The Shamrock is a popular symbol of the Trinity. It was used by St. Patrick to teach the Catholic faith in Ireland in the 400's. It has one stem and three leaves. There is One God and three Persons in the One God. Of course, nobody can understand or explain how there can be three Persons in One God.

Circle:

003

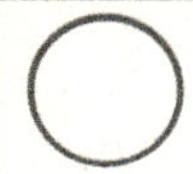

The Circle is a symbol of something that has no beginning or end. So, it is a symbol of eternity or heaven.

Three Circles:

004

Three Equal Circles are often used as a symbol of the Trinity. The three equal circles, equally spaced and locked together, express the unity, equality and eternal existence of the 3 equal Persons of the Trinity.

Triquetra:

005

On Celtic Crosses and Celtic decorations there is often a triangle-shaped figure consisting of three loops or arcs, which are interwoven. This symbol is called a Triquetra. It is made of one unbroken line into three interwoven arcs. It is a symbol of the fact that the Three Persons in One God are one and everlasting. This is probably the most beautiful of the symbols of the Blessed Trinity.

SYMBOLS OF GOD THE FATHER

Hand of God:

006

Even though there are many symbols in the catacombs outside of Rome, we find that there is only one symbol used for God the Father. It is the Hand. The hand was used for almost a thousand years after Christ. It is used many times in the Old Testament to symbolize the fact that God the Father is the Creator and Protector. Wisdom 3:1 says that the souls of the just are in the Hand of God. The hand is shown coming from the clouds and giving out blessings, or it is shown raised in a blessing and surrounded by a round halo inside of which are three rays. This symbolizes the divinity and the three Persons in God.

Eye of God:

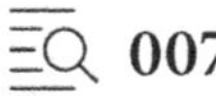
007

Another symbol of God the Father is an eye in an equilateral triangle. It is a symbol of God's power to see everything and know everything.

SYMBOLS OF CHRIST

I.N.R.I.:

008

These letters stand for the Latin words, Jesus Nazarenus, Rex Iudaeorum or Jesus of Nazareth, The King of the Jews. Pilot ordered that this sign be put on the cross to which Jesus was nailed.

ihs:

009

This is a monogram (sign) for the Name of Jesus using the first three letters of the name written in Greek – ΙΗΣΟΥΣ. This was later misunderstood as a Latin abbreviation I.H.S. for Jesus Hominum Salvator, which is translated as Jesus, the Savior of Men.

Chi Rho:
010

This symbol looks like the letter "P" with an "X" at the lower half of the "P". It is called the Chi Rho. The Chi (X) and the Rho (P) pronounced key-roe, are the first two letters of the Greek word CHRISTOS (Christ). It is a symbol of the name of Christ, the Redeemer. It began to be used by Christians after the time of Emperor Constantine (early 300's) and is a popular symbol today.

Alpha & Omega:
011

The Alpha and Omega are the first and last letters of the Greek alphabet, and the symbol is taken from the Book of Revelation 1:8; I am the Alpha and the Omega, the Beginning and the End, says the Lord God. If a symbol for Christ is drawn along with the Alpha and the Omega, it symbolizes that Christ is the beginning and the end of all things.

Lamb:
012

The Lamb is one of the most beloved symbols of Jesus Christ. The term Lamb is applied to Him 28 times in the Scriptures. Lambs were sacrificed in the Old Testament, and the prophets foretold that the Lamb would be slain for the sins of all the peoples. John the Baptist pointed to Jesus Christ and said, "Behold the Lamb of God Who takes away the sin of the world." (John 1:29). This is said at every Mass. Early Christian art shows the lamb alone. Later the lamb is shown standing on a hill. Four rivers flow from the hill, a symbol of the Four Gospels. At times the Lamb is shown on a book, which has seven seals. This is described in the Book of Revelation 5:1-7 by St. John. At other times, the Lamb is shown with a banner of victory and a cross on it. This is a symbol of the risen Savior, who conquered sin and death, and is our standard bearer.

Good Shepherd:

013

Jesus is known as the Good Shepherd. He stands with a sheep, or with a lamb, on His shoulders or in His arms. It is a symbol of Christ bringing home the sinner. The symbol comes from John 10:11, "I am the good shepherd." This the oldest symbol of Jesus Christ as the good shepherd.

Fish:

014

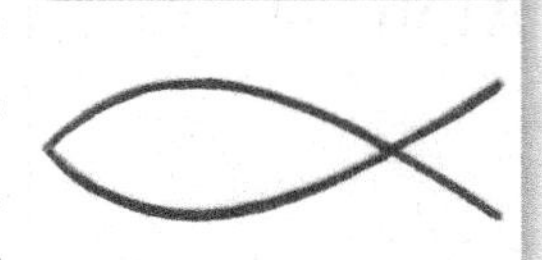

The fish is widely recognized in Christianity. This symbol was used from the very beginning of the Church. Christians would use it to identify each other. There are two meanings for it: First, it may represent Christ Himself, especially in the Eucharist; Second, it may represent a newly baptized soul. The Greek word for fish is ICHTHUS. Each of these letters begins a Greek word in the title of the Redeemer. They are, in English, Jesus Christ, Son of God, Savior.

Risen Christ, Standard Bearer:

015

In scenes of the Resurrection of Jesus Christ from the dead He is depicted as holding a banner or standard with a cross on it. This is a symbol of the fact that Jesus Christ is Our Standard Bearer or leader through the cross to the resurrection found in Acts 5:31.

King (Crown):

016

Jesus Christ said, "I am a King", so the symbol of the crown is used. The crown is a symbol of sovereignty and victory, and a symbol of Christ, who is ruler of all people. In the catacombs the crown is a symbol of the victory of the martyrs who received the crown of everlasting life. In the catacombs there are drawings of martyrs offering their crowns to Jesus Christ or receiving a crown from Him. This reminds us of James 1:12, that for those who love God, He has promised to give the crown of life.

Heart:

017

Catholics have pictures of Jesus with His Heart visible. The Heart of Jesus, which is shown in this way, is a symbol of the love of Jesus for all people. The heart is said to be the dwelling place of the whole interior life of man. The honor given to the Heart of Jesus is not directed to His Heart separate from Him but is essentially honor of Jesus Himself. The beginning of this devotion to the Sacred Heart is to be found in the Old and New Testaments, and the early writers of the Church, or the Fathers of the Church.

(1) The love of God for mankind is like the love of a mother for her child, Isaiah 49:14-15, and like the love of a husband for his wife, Hosea 1-2.
(2) In John's Gospel 7:37-39, at the Feast of Tabernacles, Jesus promised a fountain of living water from within Him.

The pierced Heart of Jesus is often shown pouring living water of grace upon His Church. The Sacred Heart reminds us of the compassion and mercy of Jesus Christ. This devotion was promoted strongly after St. Margaret Mary Alocoque had her visions of the Sacred Heart in 1674 and 1675 and also by St. Faustina in 1931-1938.

Scepter:

018

There are drawings of Jesus Christ sitting on a throne holding a scepter or a thin rod. On the top of the rod is a ball with a cross. This is a symbol of the kingly authority of the Redeemer of mankind. The Scepter was a symbol of power and dignity long before Christianity. In the Old Testament Book of Numbers 24:17, there is the prophecy that a scepter shall spring up or rise up from Israel.

Vine:

019

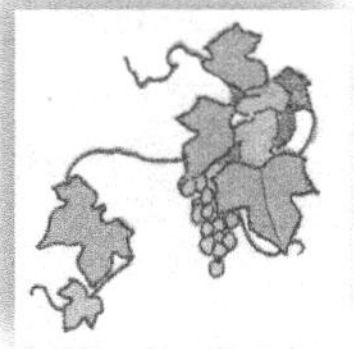

Jesus Christ said, "I am the vine, you are the branches," in Jn 15:5. The vine is often drawn in the catacombs and is a symbol of our union with Christ. Jesus is the head and source of divine life to the members of the

Church. We are the living branches who became attached to the vine at our baptism. While we live attached to the true vine, Jesus Christ, we live a supernatural life and grow strong with each Holy Communion we receive.

SYMBOLS OF THE HOLY SPIRIT

020

Dove:

In the Old Testament, long before anyone knew about the fact that there are three Persons in God, the Spirit of God was not thought of as a separate Person, but as the power of God, a part of Him, like His arm or foot. In reading the story about Noah and the Flood, the dove was the symbol of peace restored between God and man. In all four Gospels the Holy Trinity is revealed at the Baptism of Jesus. The Holy Spirit appears as a dove. Statements which Jesus made point out that the Holy Spirit is equal to the Father and the Son, and so must be a Person. Artists have so little to go on that they still use the Old Testament dove as a symbol. Up to the Middle Ages the Holy Spirit was sometimes painted as a human figure, but Pope Benedict XIV (1740-1758) decreed that this kind of representation of the Holy Spirit was unacceptable, and so it quickly faded away.

021

Wind:

Another symbol for the Holy Spirit is Wind.

In Acts 2:2, the Apostles and Mary were together praying for the Holy Spirit to come. And suddenly from the sky a noise came like a strong driving wind which was heard through the house where they were seated.

022

Fire:

Yet another symbol of the Holy Spirit is Fire (Acts 2:3-4). Tongues of fire appeared, parted, came to rest on each of them and filled them with the Holy Spirit.

In a Church, the Holy Spirit is often depicted as hovering over the altar. It is a reminder that the Holy Spirit brings about the changing of the substance of bread and wine into the Body, Blood, Soul and Divinity of Jesus Christ. If the Holy Spirit is over the pulpit, it is a reminder that the Holy Spirit inspires the preacher to proclaim the truth of the Gospel with courage. He is depicted as coming down upon the bread and wine and the preacher.

SYMBOLS OF THE GOSPELS

Each of the Gospels has a symbol. The symbols for the four Evangelists, Matthew, Mark, Luke and John, are taken from a vision which Ezekiel had and is recorded in Ezekiel 1:10-11. In the 4th century St. Jerome took these four figures from Ezekiel as representing the four evangelists who would spread the Gospel, or Good News, about the Messiah, the one who would deliver all mankind from the chains of sin. The faces of each of the four creatures which had wings and human form had the face of a man, the face of a lion, the face of an ox, and the face of an eagle.

Winged Man – Matthew:

023

The Winged Man is a symbol of St. Matthew. His Gospel begins with the account of the human ancestry of Jesus, and it also emphasizes the humanity and the kingly character of the Redeemer of the world.

Winged Lion – Mark:

024

The Winged Lion is a symbol of St. Mark. In Mk 1:3, he began his Gospel with John the Baptist who was like a roaring lion in the wilderness shouting to prepare the way of the Lord and make straight His paths.

Winged Ox – Luke:

025

The Winged Ox is a symbol of St. Luke. In the Old Testament the ox was a symbol of sacrifice, and St. Luke's Gospel emphasizes the priestly office and the sacrificial death of Jesus Christ.

Winged Eagle – John:

026

The Winged Eagle is a symbol of St. John, the Evangelist. The eagle is a bird which soars high into the sky. John's Gospel gives us a view of the height, depth and vastness of God's love and compassion for every human soul.

OTHER SYMBOLS

Pelican:

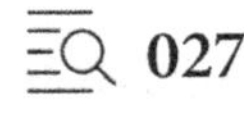 027

The pelican is a white bird with a long beak which has a sack that functions as a storage area for small fish which it feeds to its young. In the feeding of the young, the bird presses the sack against its neck in such a way that it seems to open its breast with its beak. The reddish color of the feathers on its breast and the reddish tip of its beak gave rise to the idea that the pelican drew blood from its own heart to feed its young. This story was used as a symbol of self-sacrifice and therefore of Jesus Christ giving His Blood on Mount Calvary in order to save mankind, and each day in the sacrifice of the Mass where He gives us His Flesh to eat and His Blood to drink. Jesus said in Jn 6 that the bread that He will give us is His flesh for the life of the world. From the late Middle Ages, this symbol of the Eucharist was popular in Christian art on chalices, tabernacle doors, and altars.

Phoenix:

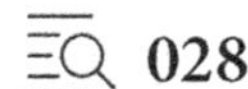 028

The Phoenix is another bird which is used in Christian art. The ancient Egyptians had a legend about a bird, which lived in the desert for 500 to a thousand years. It would set a fire with its own wings and burn itself to death but would rise from its own ashes in youthful freshness.

The early Fathers of the Church used this story to teach the resurrection of Christ and the resurrection of our bodies to life everlasting, and so we use the phoenix as a symbol of resurrection and immortality. There are drawings of the phoenix in the catacombs dating from the 2nd and 3rd centuries.

Peacock:

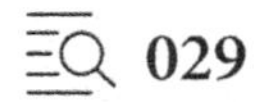 **029**

The Peacock is widely recognized as a Christian symbol. The Roman mother goddess, Juno, held the Peacock sacred, but the early Christians adopted it and drew it in the catacombs as a symbol of immortality. It was thought that the flesh of the peacock did not decay, and it shed its feathers each year to take on more beautiful feathers. In this way it became a symbol of the resurrection and life everlasting. The peacock is often drawn standing on a globe. This is a symbol of the victory of the immortal soul over the world. At times, the peacock is shown as drinking from a vase. This is a symbol of the soul refreshing itself from the living waters of the sacraments.

Dove – Peace:

030

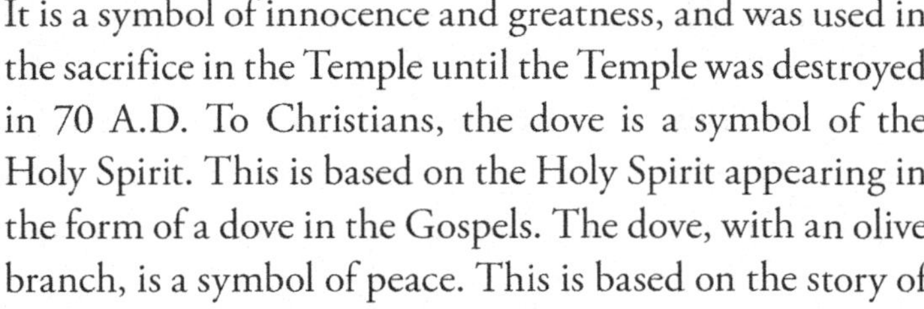

It is a symbol of innocence and greatness, and was used in the sacrifice in the Temple until the Temple was destroyed in 70 A.D. To Christians, the dove is a symbol of the Holy Spirit. This is based on the Holy Spirit appearing in the form of a dove in the Gospels. The dove, with an olive branch, is a symbol of peace. This is based on the story of Noah sending a dove out from the Ark. When it returned with an olive branch, Noah took it as a symbol that God was no longer angry, and peace and life could return to earth after the Flood.

Palm:

031

The palm is a symbol of victory. The early Christians adopted the symbol of their spiritual victory over sin and the world. It also became a symbol of their great Hall of Famers, the martyrs. In the Book of Revelation 7:9, St. John saw a great multitude before the throne and the Lamb, clothed in white robes, with palm branches in their hands. Originally, people went in procession from Bethany to the city of Jerusalem, as Jesus Christ did on that first Palm Sunday. Those people carried palm branches or olive branches, the two most common trees in Palestine found in Jn 12:1-15. The celebrations of Palm Sunday spread throughout Europe, and then throughout the world, and those in procession celebrated with local versions of palms; for example, cedar branches, flowers, and so on, whatever grew locally. It was Palm Sunday, April 2, 1513, when Ponce De Leon, the Spanish explorer, arrived in the territory now known as the State of Florida. He named it La Florida because flowers were so plentiful, and flowers were substituted for palms in his native country of Spain on Palm Sunday, the Catholic Feast of Pascua Florida.

Water:

Water is a symbol for many different things.

Here are a few examples of water's symbolism:

> Water cleanses us from filth and impurity. Consequently, water is used as a symbol of interior cleanliness and purification.
>
> Water is a symbol of life because man, animals and plants need water in order to live.
>
> Water, moving as a river after a heavy rain is, for the people of the Middle East, a symbol of the majesty and power of God.
>
> Water, for people in dry lands, is a symbol of happiness, and of God's blessing.
>
> Water, in the form of stormy seas in which ships are tossed about and sailors are terrified, is a symbol of terrible danger.

For Christians, water is used mostly as a symbol of purification and life. Water is used in baptism as a symbol of cleansing the soul of all sins. Non-Christians use water also. Hindus consider it very important to bathe in and drink the water of the Ganges River in India as a way to enjoy rest after death. The ancient Egyptians performed ritual washings before entering into a holy place, also to ceremonially cleanse some objects like a city or house. The ancient Babylonians poured water on people whom they believed to have demons in them. The Greeks purified themselves with the seawater. The Romans required washing before handling the household gods, and they sprinkled water on houses, temples and whole cities. The Islamic people wash before their daily prayers. So, Christianity is not the only religion which performs the ritual use of water.

In the Old Testament, water was used in rites of purification. Aaron and his sons had to purify themselves before entering the tabernacle. Objects, such as garments, had to be washed completely. There is no indication in the Old Testament that water had to be blessed with a prayer as it is in the Catholic Church today. In the New Testament, John the Baptist prepared the way of the Lord by baptizing with water. Baptizing with water was performed by several Jewish religious groups at that time. The baptism of John was not the Sacrament of Baptism, but an outward sign of one's inner sorrow for one's own sins. Also, Jesus washed the feet of His disciples with water at the Last Supper.

Holy Water:

Long before Christianity, people knew the effects of water on vegetation and life. They looked upon water as being magical because it made vegetation grow and kept life going. Christians Christianized water. In many pagan religions and in the Jewish religion, a water ritual was common. It was an external sign of internal purification before approaching the presence of God. (We bless ourselves with Holy Water as we enter a Church where Jesus is present.) This custom was adopted by early Christians. The use of Holy Water is a reminder of our baptism and the promises we made during that ceremony. Salt is usually added to ordinary water during the blessing of the water. This custom came from the story of the miraculous cure of the poisonous well where the prophet Elisha used salt to purify it in 2 Kings 2:19–22. Today people are encouraged to bless their homes, property, fields and themselves with Holy Water. Water is blessed by a bishop, priest or deacon who solemnly imposes God's blessing upon those who use it. This is called Holy Water. It is used as a sacramental and obtains favors from God through the prayers of the Church offered for those who make use of it. One of the earliest mentions we have in the Catholic Church about the use of blessed water, or Holy Water, is found in the Acts of Peter, which was written in the 2nd century and is not included in the Bible. Pope Alexander I (107-115 A.D.) gave guidelines for blessing water and mixing it with salt for blessing homes. By the 6th century, the practice of using Holy Water was well established. The modern formula of blessing water is based on the writings of Alcuin, who died in 804. Holy Water is used frequently to bless people, objects and places in order to protect them from evil. People use it when entering a church as a way to purify themselves before they approach the presence of God.

Salt:

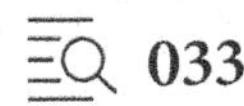
033

Salt has been used a great deal in the Church. Salt is blessed and sprinkled over areas much like Holy Water. Salt was of great importance for thousands of years. The world's major trading routes were built for salt. The Via Salaria, or Salt Way, for example, is an important highway in Italy. It was built originally by Roman soldiers for camel caravans, which carried sea salt inland from Rome's port of Ostia on the Tyrrhenian Sea. Roman guards lined the Via Salaria to protect the caravans from being attacked because salt was so precious. The soldiers were paid with salt, and that is where we get the word salary. If a soldier was a poor worker he was said to be not worth his salt. At times salt has been worth as much as gold. Salt is absolutely necessary for the body. Human life develops in amniotic fluid, which has a salt content similar to that of the sea. The average adult body contains 250 grams of salt. Salt performs many functions inside the body. We cry salty tears, and our bodies perspire salt. Without salt we would die. Salt symbolizes purity and the making holy of something. Greeks and Romans used it in sacrifices by placing it on the head of the victim. Superstitions surrounded the spilling of salt. For the Romans, it was bad luck to spill salt. Salt, in the Bible, represents wisdom. Our Lord calls His apostles the salt of the earth, because through them the Gospel would be spread all over the world. Salt is used to preserve, and so was used as a symbol of preserving from sin.

Oil:

034

The Church uses three holy oils:

Chrism – this is a mixture of olive oil and balm, which is blessed by the bishop at the Chrism Mass during Holy Week.

Oil of Catechumens – this is olive oil, which has been blessed.

Oil of the sick – this is also blessed olive oil. Since ancient times, oil was used as a seasoning or preservative, as a fuel for lamps, and as a source of healing for wounds.

The most frequently mentioned use of oil in the Bible is that of anointing, the anointing of priests, prophets and kings. To anoint a guest on the head was a sign of honor. People were anointed in preparation for burial. Oil was used to beautify. Jesus instituted the Sacrament of the Anointing of the Sick. This is mentioned in James 5:14. Nowadays, oil is used in administering the sacraments of Baptism, Confirmation, Holy Orders, Anointing of the Sick, and in Consecration of the Altar and walls in a new church. Persons were anointed, but also objects were anointed. In Gen 28:18-19, Jacob poured oil on the stone at Bethel as a sign of consecration. The shield of a warrior might be anointed. Oil was used in sacrifice. These uses of oil in the Bible gave rise to its use in the Church. The word oil was used also to mean other things; for example, soft words, joy, abundance, the influence of the Holy Spirit.

Ashes:

035

Catholics begin Lent on Ash Wednesday when they put ashes on their foreheads. Ancient peoples used ashes for religious, medical or magical purposes. The ancient ashes were from plants, animals, or human bodies, which had been burned. The ashes used today in churches are the ashes of palm branches, which were used the previous Palm Sunday and then burned. Use of ashes in the Old Testament signified mortality, repentance, sorrow and worthlessness. Ashes were sprinkled on the head, or covered the body. Sometimes people sat in or lie in the ashes, and people even ate ashes. The use of ashes in Christian Liturgy is taken from the Jewish custom, and is used only on Ash Wednesdays when people go around with ashes in the form of a cross on their foreheads. This custom has been universally practiced since the Synod of Benevento in 1091. A century earlier, it was practiced by the Anglo-Saxons. Ashes were first used as a sign of private penance and later introduced into the liturgy. They were also used to bring out sympathy for the person wearing them, and consequently people would pray for them.

Incense:

036

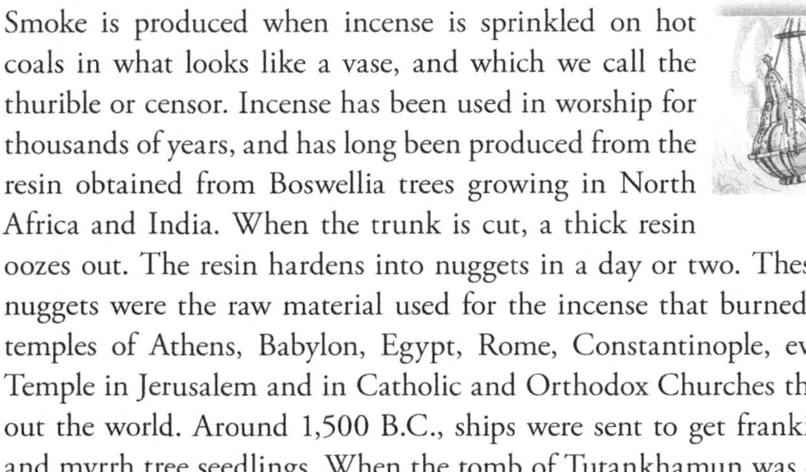

Smoke is produced when incense is sprinkled on hot coals in what looks like a vase, and which we call the thurible or censor. Incense has been used in worship for thousands of years, and has long been produced from the resin obtained from Boswellia trees growing in North Africa and India. When the trunk is cut, a thick resin oozes out. The resin hardens into nuggets in a day or two. These resin nuggets were the raw material used for the incense that burned in the temples of Athens, Babylon, Egypt, Rome, Constantinople, even the Temple in Jerusalem and in Catholic and Orthodox Churches throughout the world. Around 1,500 B.C., ships were sent to get frankincense and myrrh tree seedlings. When the tomb of Tutankhamun was opened in the early 20th century there was a smell of myrrh still in it. The tomb had been closed around 1340 B.C., so the odor had lasted for over 3,200 years. Frankincense and myrrh are dried tree sap. They were very valuable. At the time of Christ one pound of frankincense would cost about $500 converted to today's money. A pound of myrrh would cost 8 to 10 times that amount.

Incense was not used in early Christian worship for two reasons: First, on account of its connections with pagan worship; Second, early Christian worship was held in secret, and the use of incense would be dangerous.

Incense was first used in secular settings, and later in religious services. It was used to honor kings, and the Roman Emperor. Pagans used it to worship their gods. Frankincense and myrrh were gifts which the Magi brought to Jesus Christ at His birth. In Exodus 30:1-8, Moses is told by God to make an altar of acacia wood for the burning of incense. Aaron was to do this in the morning and evening. In other places in the Old Testament incense was burned in connection with the burnt offerings of animals. In the Book of Revelation, John had a vision of heaven and of a heavenly liturgy where the twenty-four elders worship the Lamb that was slain. The elders hold gold bowls filled with incense which are the prayers of the holy ones in Rev. 5:8. In Rev. 8:3-4, an angel, holding a golden censor, is given a great quantity of incense to offer, and the smoke of the incense goes up before God with prayers. The rising smoke symbolizes prayers rising up to God. Psalm 141 says to let my prayer come like incense before you. Incense is also a sign of respect or reverence for many things during the Liturgy. The altar is incensed because it represents Christ and His Sacrifice which is made present on the altar. The Book of Gospels is incensed because it is the Word of God and Christ Himself, Who is The Word of God made flesh. The gifts on the Altar are incensed also because they are to be changed into the Body and Blood of Christ. The Eucharist is incensed because it is the Body, Blood, Soul and Divinity of Jesus Christ. This incensing is done at Mass and Benediction. The people are incensed because they are created in the image and likeness of God, and, since they are baptized, are temples of the Holy Spirit. The Easter Candle or Paschal Candle is incensed because it is a symbol of Christ, Who is the Light of the World. The Crucifix is incensed because by His death on the Cross, Jesus opened Heaven for us. At a funeral the body of a person who has died is incensed because that body was a temple of the Holy Spirit.

Medals:

Some people wear lucky charms, like a rabbit's foot. We have to admit that the rabbit's foot which some people wear was not lucky for the rabbit to whom it was attached. A religious medal is nothing like a lucky charm. A religious medal is a piece of solid substance which is usually metal, wood or plastic and is like a coin with some religious images or inscription. It is made in such a way that it can be worn around the neck. Medals are customarily blessed by the Church and intended to increase the faith and devotion of the wearer or carrier. Even in the early years of Christianity we find that medals were used. A medal dating back to the 2nd century with the images of Sts. Peter and Paul were found. A 4th century saint, St. Zeno, tells us about the custom of giving newly baptized Christians a medal in remembrance of their baptism. There are many examples of medals from the 4th through the 8th centuries. We do not find examples of religious medals honoring saints from the Middle Ages (500-1500). In the 12th century a custom began of making medals in honor of famous shrines. Religious medals, as we know them today, began to appear in the 16th century. The custom of the blessing of medals came into practice at this time too. This was started by Pope Pius V. By the 17th century, every city in Europe had its own medal with the image of Jesus, Mary, or a saint on it. Religious medals are not magic charms or amulets. The Catholic Church attributes no intrinsic power to medals, whether they are blessed or not. The medal is simply a symbol, which brings to the mind of the person who believes, his faith and his religious duties. This reminder moves him to acts of reverence to God or to Jesus Christ. The believer does not rely on help from the medal, but it helps him put his faith and hope in God.

Scapulars:

038

Sometimes Catholics wear two small pieces of cloth attached by two strings. It is called a scapular. The name scapular comes from the Latin word scapula which is a shoulder. A scapular is part of a religious habit, which consists of a length of cloth worn over the shoulders with a hole for the head. It hangs down in the front and at the back, and often extends to the ankles. It was 14 to 18 inches wide and was worn to protect the monks from rain, cold, or snow during manual labor. Sometimes a hood was attached. It symbolizes a cross carried on one's shoulders reminding one that Christ said in Lk 9:23 if anyone wishes to come after Him, let him take up his cross daily and follow Him. The scapular became part of the monastic dress at the end of the 9th century. In the 13th century it became common for some lay people to take on some of the spiritual works, penances, or prayers of the monks. That gave rise to what we call today Third Orders. The religious orders, like the Dominicans, Franciscans, and Augustinians gave these people a part of their religious habit. This very often was a scapular of the same color as the habit. The scapular was usually two pieces of cloth, one worn on the chest and the other on the back, and joined by strings, which were worn over the shoulders. At the beginning of the 16th century a small scapular was introduced, generally about 2" square. They were given to lay people who were not members of a Third Order but who were willing to take on some penances and prayers. There are at least eighteen different scapulars approved by the Church for popular devotion.

Holy Cards: 039

Inside the Bibles, prayer books, pockets and purses of Catholics, there are often cards with pictures of Jesus, Mary, the Saints and Angels on them. On the back, there is a prayer. The cards are called Holy Cards. Holy cards are hand-sized cards with printed religious images of Jesus Christ, Our Lady, a saint or angel. They are given out at some religious ceremonies or in religious education classes. The first holy cards were handmade by monks in monasteries. The Printing Press was invented in 1440, and gradually, after that, holy cards became more plentiful and popular. Modern religious holy cards got a boost when Aloys Senefelder (1771-1834) invented lithography. Now cards could be produced inexpensively. By 1825 this process was in use in the United States. Senefelder also invented chromolithography, which is a reproductive color process, and this was being used by 1840 to print holy cards. People use holy cards to remind them of Jesus, Mary, the saints and angels just as we use photographs to remind us of our loved ones.

Bells: 040

It is an old custom to ring bells in Churches. For the first 300 years of Christianity there was no way for people to announce when Mass was being celebrated, except by word of mouth, because the Catholic Church was persecuted by the Roman Empire. When Emperor Constantine passed the Edict of Milan in 313, it meant that Catholicism was no longer an illegal religion and could be practiced openly.

Different methods were used to call people to Mass and services, for example; criers, blowing of a trumpet, and the bell. The bell became the favorite method in the 5th century. Pope Sabinian (604-606) regulated the ringing of the bells to indicate the times of prayer. At first, bells were too small to be heard over distances. In the Middle Ages, the monks made bigger bells. By the 9th century, the bells were so large they could not be carried by hand so they were put on a wall or ceiling and rung by pulling a rope which was usually attached to the clapper or tongue of the bell. Some bells were attached to an axle and a rope tied to its end. Later, a wheel was introduced and the rope wound around it. Cathedrals and churches used it. By 1,000 A.D. even small churches had a bell to call parishioners to Mass and prayers.

Bells were used to call people to pray, but they were also used for another unintended purpose, to ring in a new kind of warfare. Gunpowder, which had been invented by the Chinese centuries before and used in fireworks, was introduced into Europe in the early 13th century. The Europeans turned the bells over, put in gunpowder and added shrapnel. This led to the development of the cannon and later the musket. These weapons changed the way war was waged on land and sea.

In the 11th century, Pope Gregory IX called for the ringing of a bell in the evening to remind people to pray for the Crusaders. Tradition tells us of the custom of bell ringing in the evenings to let people know it was time to cover the fires in their hearths for safety. By the 15th century, the bells were used to call people to prayer, to keep storms and danger away, and to announce curfews. The English word curfew comes from the French couvrefeu; Covrir means to cover and feu, fire. Nowadays, the most popular use of ringing bells to announce joy is the ringing of the bells in churches when a new Pope has been elected and the announcement is made, "I announce to you a great joy. We have a Pope!"

Big Candle:

041

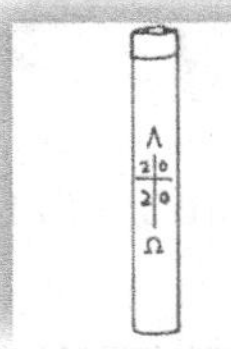

The big candle is called the Paschal Candle. It is the symbol of the risen Lord. It is lit and brought into the dark Church on Holy Saturday night and is the only light which scatters the darkness in the Church. It is a symbol of the fact that the Light of Christ overcomes and scatters the darkness of sin. This custom comes from the ancient practice of lighting and blessing a lamp, or lamps, in the evening to provide light in the darkness. As time went on, this simple ceremony of lighting the lamp was surrounded by prayers and hymns. This practice also preceded the praying of Vespers, which is the Evening Prayer of the Church. So, the custom of lighting the Paschal Candle comes from an activity that was done every day.

Candles

042

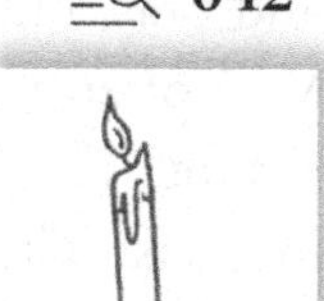

Catholics light lots of candles. They light candles around the altar and in front of statues. Candles were used by the Romans not only for lighting but also for veneration of their gods, of the dead, and of the Emperor. It was a custom, in the ancient Roman Empire, to have servants carrying candles and incense to go ahead of government officials who were walking in procession.

The Emperor Constantine, who died in 337 A.D., granted this privilege to Catholic bishops. These candles were placed near the altar after the bishop had taken his seat. Christ is the light of the world. These candles symbolized Christ and were placed near the altar even if the bishop was not present.

Candles were used by the Christians from the beginning. They were used in funeral processions. From the 3rd century, they were burned at the tombs of the dead, especially the martyrs. From the 4th and 5th century, they were lit before the relics of the saints and sacred images. Candles were used plentifully to give beauty to the churches. They were especially plentiful around the altar. From the 4th century there is evidence that candles were used at Mass. They were brought into the Church in the procession to the altar at the beginning of Mass, held up at the Gospel, then placed around the altar. In the 12th century candles began to be placed on the altar table. At first, two were placed there. As time went on the number increased until in the Middle Ages it was customary to have six tall candles lit on the altar for a solemn Mass. The 17th century brought in regulations stating the necessity of candles at Mass.

Votive Candles:

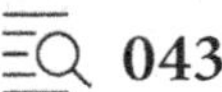

043

Votive candles are candles which are lit in front of images of Our Lord, Our Lady, or the saints.

There are two reasons for doing this: First, to honor Our Lord, Our Lady, or the Saints; Second, to symbolize our desire to have our prayer continue beyond the actual time of our presence in that particular place.

It is a continuation of our prayer. We are not able to continue to stay and pray, but the lighted candle symbolizes our wish or desire to do so. Very often people are seeking some favor from Our Lord, Our Lady, or a saint. The first votive lights were candles left burning at the tombs of martyrs. The Orthodox Jews have a similar practice. They pray at the Wailing Wall in Jerusalem, then write down their petitions on a piece of paper and place it in a crack in the wall. Their intention is that their prayer be present to God even when they cannot be completely attentive to their prayers. Buddhists also have the custom of lighting candles in front of statues.

Sanctuary Light:

044

In Catholic Churches a red light is situated fairly high on a wall or hanging from a ceiling. This red light is called a Sanctuary Light. The Sanctuary Light is kept burning near the Tabernacle to indicate that Jesus Christ is present in the Tabernacle. The Sanctuary Light is kept burning near Jesus Christ Who is present because He is the most important person present. The widespread use of a light near the Blessed Sacrament is really the work of a forgotten Benedictine monk, Eustace, Abbot of Fleay. About the year 1,200 he promoted the use of the Sanctuary Lamp during his preaching in France and England. This was a time when some Christians began to deny the Real Presence of Jesus Christ in the Eucharist. As a reaction to this, more people wanted to see and pray before the Blessed Sacrament. The use of the Sanctuary Light became so popular that church councils in the 13th century said that it was to be used everywhere. The Council of Trent (1545-63) said there should be at least one lamp burning near the Blessed Sacrament.

Sword & Book:

045

The Book is the Bible. Hebrew 4:12 says God's Word is living and effective, sharper than any two-edged sword.

Haircut:

046

Saints, like St. Francis and St. Anthony, have unusual haircuts. They are bald on the top of the head and have a circle of hair around the head. In about the 5th century a custom started called Tonsure, which involved the shaving of the head, or part of it, like the crown of thorns. The tonsure symbolized that the person wearing it was admitted into the clerical state. This practice has not been done for a while, and in the case of secular clergy, only a clip of hair was taken. Also, there was no tonsure worn after ordination. In 1972, Pope Paul VI discontinued the tonsure, and instead, entrance into the clerical state is joined with the deaconate which is an order to which men are ordained to assist priests in their care of souls.

Boat:

047

Jesus often traveled in a boat. The boat is a symbol of the Church in which the soul can sail over the troubled waters of life to the peace of eternal life. In the catacombs, the boat is drawn with a mast like a cross, and on top of the mast is a symbol of Christ or a dove. The symbol of the boat comes from the Ark of Noah which saved its occupants and of the boat which the apostles were in when Jesus saved them from the stormy Sea of Galilee.

Keys:

048

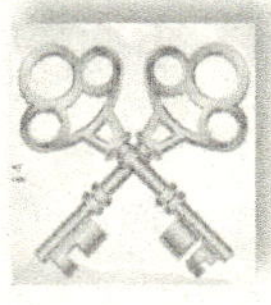

The Crossed Keys symbolize the power given to Peter when Jesus said to him, "You are Peter". In Mt. 16:18-19, He told Peter, which means rock, that upon this rock He will build His church, and the gates of hell shall not prevail against it. He entrusted the keys of the kingdom of heaven to Peter, and whatever Peter declares bound on earth shall be bound in heaven; whatever he declares loosed on earth shall be loosed in heaven.

So, Jesus appointed Peter the visible head of the Church. These keys are often referred to as The Keys of The Kingdom or The Keys of Peter. They are a symbol of the power given to Peter by Jesus Christ. The power is binding on earth and in heaven.

Anchor: 049

During the persecutions of Christians in the first 300 years by the Roman Empire the use of the cross as a symbol was not used openly. They feared desecration of the crosses or that they would be identified as Christians.

They often disguised the cross symbol as an anchor. The anchor also stood for hope and safety. Hebrews 6:19 says that hope extends beyond the veil like a sure and firm anchor. The anchor was often placed on funeral monuments as an expression of hope that the departed soul had arrived safely at the port of eternal peace.

Shell: 050

The scallop shell has always been a symbol for Baptism since it has a connection with water.

Halo or Nimbus: 051

The nimbus, or halo, is pictured as a flat disc, which stands behind the head of a holy person. It is a symbol of holiness. It may be a simple circle. It was used by the Greeks and Romans before the time of Christ as a symbol of divinity for their gods and goddesses, and especially Apollo, the sun god. The halo is usually used with the Blessed Virgin Mary, the angels or saints. If there are three rays within the circle, it is a symbol of one of the Persons of the Blessed Trinity: the Father, the Son or the Holy Spirit.

In ancient times, the nimbus was a symbol of a superior being. It was on coins of the Caesars and even the heads of the Christian emperors. Up until the 4th century, the nimbus was reserved for Jesus Christ. After that time, it was applied to the angels, the Blessed Virgin Mary, and finally the saints as a sign of holiness.

Lily: 052

The white lily symbolizes purity, innocence, and integrity. This symbol has been especially associated with the Virgin Mary and other virgin saints. In scenes of the Annunciation, the Archangel Gabriel is often portrayed as arriving with a white lily to symbolize Mary's purity. St. Joseph, too, is frequently shown with the same flower. Images of St. Cecilia, St. Clare, St. Francis of Assisi, and St. Dominic often include white lilies.

Fleur de Lis: 053

The Fleur de Lis, French for the flower of the lily, is a very popular symbol. Clovis, king of the Franks (480-511), was given the Fleur de Lis by the Blessed Virgin Mary at his Baptism when he converted to Christianity. The Fleur de Lis has been associated with the French crown.

CROSS

Cross:

The Cross is a symbol of Christianity. In the first 3 centuries Christians were persecuted by the Romans and rarely, if ever, displayed crosses. Before the time of Christ, the cross was a shameful thing, an instrument of torture and capital punishment. Christians did not want to display the way Christ died. They emphasized His resurrection. To display a cross during these times of persecution would be dangerous. Also, the first Christians were influenced by the Old Testament admonition against making graven images to gods.

In the 4th century, things changed. In 312 A. D. the Roman Emperor, Constantine, was trying to get control of the whole empire. Before the decisive battle just outside of Rome, it is said he that saw a cross in the sky and the words, "In this sign, you will conquer." Constantine won the battle and attributed the victory to the cross. His troops put a cross on their shields, and within a few years the cross in the shape of a Chi Rho began to appear on Roman coins. As time went on, the cross became less associated with the death of criminals and more with the suffering and victory of Christ. Constantine's mother, Helena, discovered the true Cross on her pilgrimage to Jerusalem, and more and more honor was given to the Cross.

By the 5th century, the Christians overcame their unwillingness to display images of the cross. A bare cross was increasingly used as a sign of the Lord's victory over sin and death. These crosses did not have the crucified Christ on them. They were often made of precious metals and decorated with jewels.

From the 6th century onward, there were more and more depictions of Christ on the cross. In the 8th and 9th centuries, artists began to depict the actual death of Jesus on the Cross. Around the 11th century, crucifixes as we see them today, a cross with a separate corpus or body attached to it, began to be made in Europe. Usually Christ on the Cross was living, open-eyed, with head up and sometimes wearing a crown.

During the Middle Ages, the Church's attitude towards pain and suffering shifted. Now Christians were encouraged to accept sickness and bodily pain as a form of discipline given by God for their spiritual strengthening. Wars, crusades, plagues and other sufferings were common at that time. In the 12th century, crucifixes began reflecting the new emphasis on suffering. Christ was depicted as dead on the cross. By the middle of the 13th century, the Dominicans and Franciscans preached devotion to the suffering Christ. The glorified Christ was set aside. The suffering and death of Christ were depicted on the cross. During the 14th century, the Black Death devastated Europe. The sick and dying found consolation in meditating on the crucifixion knowing that God Himself had suffered too.

The 2nd Vatican Council (1962-65) reemphasized the unity of Christ's suffering and resurrection. Artists were encouraged to depict these on the crucifixes.

TYPES OF CROSSES

There are many types of crosses and there is a great deal of symbolism attached to each of them.

San Damiano Cross:

054

It is the cross in front of which St. Francis of Assisi was praying when he heard a voice telling him, "Go, rebuild My Church." Francis then began a life of poverty and dedication to Jesus

Christ. He founded the three Franciscan Orders. The crucifix was probably painted in Umbria in the 12th century.

Swastika:

055

The swastika is called Crux Gammata and was used in pre-Christian times as a symbol of good fortune. This symbol is in the shape of a Greek Cross with the arms bent clockwise or counterclockwise at right angles with one arm perpendicular to the other arm.

Ankh:

056

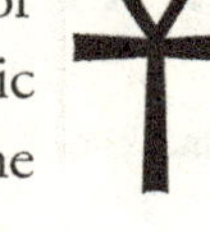

The Ankh is called Crux Ansata from the Latin which is a cross with a handle. It was used in pre-Christian times and was for the ancient Egyptians a symbol of eternal life. The early Coptic Christians in Egypt adapted it into the Crux Ansata. It is like the Tau cross with a loop.

Tau:

057

It resembles the Latin letter T. It is called Tau because it is the 19th letter of the Greek alphabet and the Greek word for our letter T. This cross was adopted by the Egyptian Christians and is connected with St. Anthony of the Desert (251-356 A.D.). It is the symbol of St. Francis of Assisi and the three Franciscan Orders. It is called the Crux Commissa which is Latin for connected cross.

Eastern:

058

This cross is used in the Eastern churches.

It has three bars:

The top bar symbolizes the title which Pilate had placed there, The King of the Jews, found in Mk 15:26;

The middle bar is where Christ's hands were crucified;

And the third bar at the bottom is for the footrest. This third bar always points towards the left to the side of the good thief.

Jerusalem:

059

It has a cross in the center which is surrounded by four smaller Greek crosses. These five represent the five wounds of Christ. This cross is the symbol of the Latin Kingdom of Jerusalem which was established after the First Crusade (1095-1099).

Latin:

060

Tradition tells us that this was the type of cross used to execute Jesus Christ.

Greek:

061

This cross has four limbs of equal length. It is called Greek because it was largely used in medieval Greek Architecture.

Maltese:

062

This has four equal limbs which spread out into a triangular shape. It was used in the Crusades as a symbol of the Christian warrior. It is called the Maltese Cross because it was the badge of the military and the religious order of the Knights of Malta. The eight sharp points of the cross symbolize the eight Beatitudes which Jesus spoke about in the Sermon on the Mount found in Mt 5:3-11.

St. Andrew's:

063

This is in the form of the letter X. Andrew, an Apostle of Christ, was crucified on a cross of this description at Patra in Greece. He had requested this type of cross because he felt that he was not worthy to die on the same type of cross on which Christ died.

Celtic:

 **064**

The Celtic Cross is closely linked to the Church in Ireland and other Celtic areas. It is said that it was introduced into Ireland by St. Patrick (d. 461) who used it to explain the victory of Christ over the pagan sun god. The sun is in the background and the cross is in the front.

St. Brigid's:

065

The story which gives rise to this cross tells us that Brigid of Ireland, who was well known for her charity, took care of a pagan chieftain who was ill. While he slept Brigid wove a cross with some of the straw from the floor. When the chieftain saw the cross, he asked her why she made it. She told him about Jesus dying on the Cross at Calvary. The chieftain became a Catholic because of her weaving of the cross. He converted and was Baptized probably on account of Brigid's prayers. St. Brigid's Cross is hung in many homes in Ireland.

Patriarchal:

066

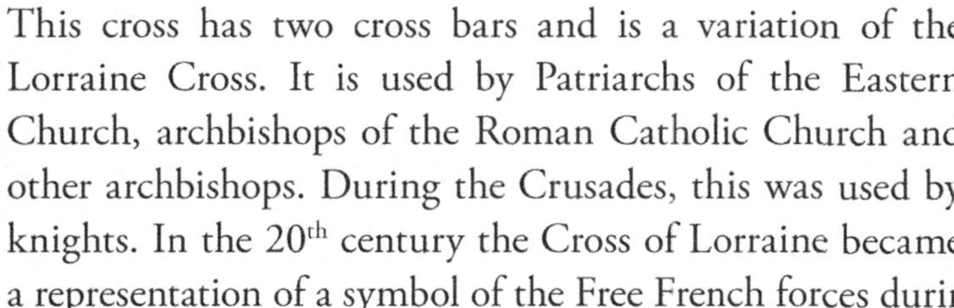

This cross has two cross bars and is a variation of the Lorraine Cross. It is used by Patriarchs of the Eastern Church, archbishops of the Roman Catholic Church and other archbishops. During the Crusades, this was used by knights. In the 20th century the Cross of Lorraine became a representation of a symbol of the Free French forces during World War II. The Patriarchal Cross is on the flags of several countries.

Crucifix and Skull and Crossbones

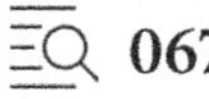 **067**

There is skull and crossbones at the foot of some crucifixes. Origen, an early Church writer who was born in Egypt in 185 A.D., said that the cross of Christ was set up on the place where the bones of Adam were buried. He was making the point that the sacrifice of Jesus Christ was offered to make up for Adam's sin.

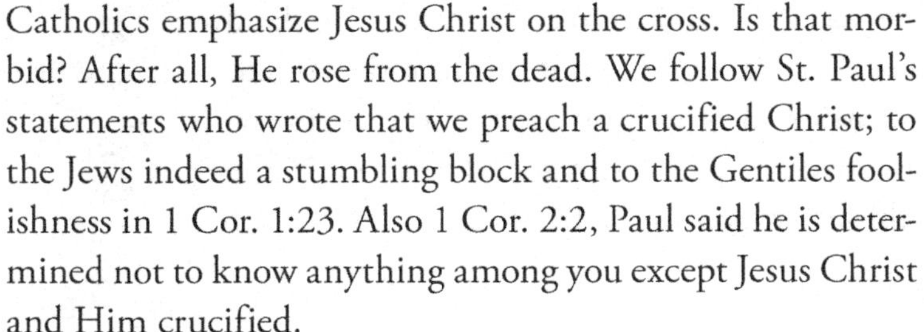

Jesus on the Cross:

068

Catholics emphasize Jesus Christ on the cross. Is that morbid? After all, He rose from the dead. We follow St. Paul's statements who wrote that we preach a crucified Christ; to the Jews indeed a stumbling block and to the Gentiles foolishness in 1 Cor. 1:23. Also 1 Cor. 2:2, Paul said he is determined not to know anything among you except Jesus Christ and Him crucified.

We must also keep in mind that Jesus Christ is drawn by artists in many ways: as a lamb, an infant in His mother's arms, a spirit-filled man engaged in public ministry, a shepherd, and also the triumphant risen Lord. However, the crucifixion is drawn more than any of these. Why? Because that was the Father's plan for His Son, Jesus Christ.

The crucifix, a cross with Jesus's body on it, reminds us of the price of our salvation and God's infinite love for us. God so loved the world that He gave His only Son to death on a cross found in Jn 3:16.

A crucifix helps us to remember that the sacrifice of Christ and the sacrifice of the Eucharist are one single sacrifice (*Catechism of the Catholic Church* 1545 – 1545 refers to the paragraph). During Mass, Jesus, through the priest, offers Himself to the Father for us.

PART TWO

HEAVENLY FRIENDS IN CHRIST

Our Lady in Blue: 069

Usually when we see an image or statue of the Blessed Virgin Mary, she is wearing blue. Blue has been traditionally associated with the Blessed Virgin Mary since 500 A.D. Byzantine artists used the color blue in connection with Our Lady. They held the Blessed Virgin in such esteem that they used the most luxurious color they could get.

Our Lady with a Snake at Her Feet:

The snake is the serpent which was referred to in the Book of Genesis Chapter 3. Adam and Eve confessed that they had eaten the fruit of the tree. God first condemned the serpent, who tempted Eve, then condemned Eve, and finally condemned Adam. The statues and pictures take their idea from the condemnation of the serpent in the Book of Genesis. "I will put enmity between you and the woman, and between your offspring and hers; he will strike at your head while you strike at his heel." (Gen 3:15). The artists took this as a prophesy and portrayed Mary, the new Eve, crushing the head of the serpent or devil by stepping on him.

The Seven Swords in Mary's Heart: 070

These swords symbolize the Seven Sorrows of Mary.

They are:

The prophecy of Simeon (Luke 2:25-35);
The flight into Egypt (Matthew 2:13-15);
Loss of the Child Jesus for three days (Luke 2:41-50);
Mary meets Jesus on His way to Calvary (Luke 23:27-31, John 19:17);
Crucifixion and Death of Jesus (John 19:25-30);
The body of Jesus being taken from the Cross (Psalm 130, Luke 23:50-54, John 19:31-37);

The burial of Jesus (Isaiah 53:8, Luke 23:50-56, John 19:38-42, Mark 15:40-47).

Apparitions:

071

People in the Catholic Church often talk about apparitions or visions of Jesus, Mary, angels, or saints. Whenever someone claims to have an apparition, the Church requires proof because hallucinations and illusions are common. Also, there may be evil spirits involved. In the Bible, there are many examples of true apparitions from God; for example, the Archangel Gabriel appearing to Mary.

Angels:

072

From the 4th century artists have drawn angels as having wings.

The artists wanted to show:

The dexterity or readiness in the use or control of the mental powers of the angels;
The speed of thought and movement of the angels;
The loftiness of angels.

Communion of Saints:

073

The Communion of Saints is the union that exists between the saints in heaven, the souls in Purgatory and the faithful who are living on earth. These three groups make up the Church. The Church Triumphant consists of the saints who are living in triumph in heaven. The Church Suffering consists of the souls in Purgatory who are being purified of their venial sins or the effects of their mortal sins. The Church Militant consists of the faithful people here on earth who are fighting to win heaven. The Communion of Saints is affirmed in the Apostles' Creed. It is mentioned in the Second Council of Nicaea in 787, in the Council of Florence (1431-1445), and the Council of Trent (1545-1563).

Saints: 074

The Church has recognized as saints those who gave heroic witness to Christ: first the martyrs who died for the faith and then those whose lives bore witness to the faith. After those people died, a spontaneous veneration grew up among those who knew them, lived with them and knew their lives.

Bishops would canonize their parishioners after their death if they were deemed worthy. As the Church grew and spread, it became necessary for the Pope to approve of this spontaneous veneration. The first saint canonized by a pope, Pope John XV, was St. Ulrich of Augsburg in 993. In 1170 Pope Alexander III required that the canonization of all saints had to be approved by Rome. In 1234, it became law by Pope Gregory IX.

Today the procedure for canonization, or to be declared a saint, is a long one. It entails investigation into a person's virtues, writings, reputation for holiness and miracles which are to be attached to the intercessions made to the person since the time of the person's death. One miracle is needed to be declared Blessed, and another miracle is needed to be declared Saint.

When Catholics pray to the saints, we are not trying to bypass God as if He were too busy or not interested in us. Instead, we are asking a holy person to pray to God for us and with us. We do not worship the saints; we only worship God. The saints are our Hall of Famers. They are our heroes. They are our champions who have won the race and gotten into heaven.

Names: 075

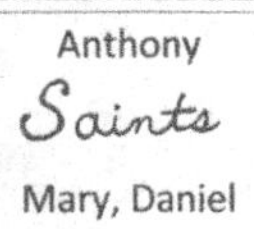

It has been a tradition in the Catholic Church to choose a saint's name for a child at Baptism. The child learns stories about this saint and tries to imitate the saint's virtues. The child also is encouraged to pray to this saint and seek the saint's help. The saint is called the child's Patron Saint. Nowadays in many countries a person has a surname and a given name. Surnames, or family names, came about in different ways.

It could be that a man was named for the work he did; for example, Carpenter, Smith, Taylor, etc., or he may be named after the place in which he lived. Sometimes the word son was added to the name of the father; for example, Williamson. Sometimes people changed their names when they emigrated to avoid danger or to make the name easier to pronounce or to spell. In many countries the family name came from the father, but in Spanish speaking countries the custom is to add the mother's family name after the father's surname. Given names are often derived from Greek and Latin words, from the Bible, from famous people, or from nature.

The practice of giving children the name of a Christian saint dates from the 4th century. Children were given the names of Apostles, saints, martyrs or confessors. This practice had spread throughout Europe by the thirteenth century.

Ireland did not adopt this practice. Consequently, there are no Christian names found in ancient Irish documents. Irish parents considered it to be irreverent to give their children the names of saints. But in the 13th century the practice on the continent of Europe took hold in Ireland also. All Christian nations, except Spanish-speaking people, do not give their children the sacred name of Jesus. However, Spanish-speaking boys are often called by that name. Out of reverence for the name of Peter, no pope has chosen that name for himself. In Ireland, the Blessed Virgin Mary is given a special name, Muire, and the name is never given to anybody else. In Spanish-speaking countries, girls are often given the Spanish name of Mary, Maria, and also some of Mary's titles and attributes; for example, Dolores (Our Lady of Sorrows), Concepcion (The Immaculate Conception), etc.

Infant of Prague: 076

In some Catholic Churches and homes there is a statue of the child Jesus with a crown on His head and a globe with a cross on it in the left hand symbolizing that Christ is ruler and redeemer of the whole world. Jesus redeemed the world by the cross. The right hand, raised in blessing with the two rings on the fingers, symbolizes earth and sky, and Jesus Christ is Lord of heaven and earth.

The original statue was once given to St. Teresa of Availa. It is called the Infant of Prague. The statue was made of wood and covered with wax in Spain in the 16th century. It is 19 inches (48 cm) in height. At that time there was strong devotion to Christ's holy childhood. The statue was brought to Prague, Czechoslovakia and given to a Carmelite monastery. In 1630, the monastery was invaded, the monks driven out, and the statue thrown behind the altar with its fingers broken off. It lay there for seven years. The monks returned, found the statue and restored it.

Statue of St. Joseph: 077

Some people, who want to sell or buy a house, bury a statue of St. Joseph near the house. This is done by some Catholics and by some who are not Catholic. Realtors are probably more familiar with this than priests. It is not known where this custom comes from, but it is mostly attributed to St. Teresa of Avila (1515 -1582), the Spanish mystic and doctor of the Church. Tradition tells us that St. Teresa traveled through Europe looking for land where she could build Carmelite convents. She encouraged her nuns to pray to St. Joseph for guidance. One time she found suitable property but had no money to buy it and no place to stay. The nuns began to pray to St. Joseph for funds, and they buried a medal of St. Joseph on the property to keep it safe from thieves. Shortly after the nuns prayed, a buyer bought the land and built a convent for them. St. Teresa dug up the medal and built a shrine to St. Joseph in thanksgiving for his intercession. Some people place a statue of St. Joseph on their property and pray to him to intercede for them to buy or sell their property. That is acceptable.

In the late 1800's, Saint André of Montreal constantly sought the intercession of St. Joseph in matters of property. In the 1900's, Dorothy Day did this also. She and Peter Mauren, a French immigrant and former Christian Brother, set up houses of hospitality in honor of St. Joseph.

St. Joseph's Altar: 078

The St. Joseph's Altar began in the Middle Ages in Sicily when there was a lengthy famine and drought. The people prayed to St. Joseph, the Patron Saint of Italy, for help. The rains did come, and the crops flourished. In thanksgiving the people brought their food as an offering to St. Joseph. The St. Joseph Altar has three levels which represent the Blessed Trinity. A Statue of St. Joseph is given a place of honor on it. White cloths and numerous flowers cover the altar. The finest wine, fruits, and vegetables are prepared along with twelve fish for the Twelve Apostles. No meat is served because this is celebrated during Lent on or around March 19th, the Feast Day of St. Joseph. Everyone is invited to share in prayers and the feasting. There is a basket on the altar in which to place written prayer intentions.

A bowl of green fava beans is often placed on the altar and guests are invited to take home a lucky bean. This custom arose from one of the famines in Sicily where the fava bean was used as fodder for cattle. The farmers cooked these beans and ate them in order to survive. Today, the fava bean is looked upon as being a delicacy. These beans, along with all the food on the altar, are blessed.

Putting together a St. Joseph's Altar involves many weeks of hard work of baking cookies and different kinds of bread which are made in different shapes and sizes. Children are dressed as members of the Holy Family, angels and saints, and these are served first at the meal. Then the guests are served. When the meal is over the remainder of the food is brought to the needy.

Statue of St. Anthony & the Child Jesus: 079

St. Anthony died in 1231, and yet there are statues with St. Anthony holding the Child Jesus in his arms. About 11 miles from Padua, Italy, Count Tiso built a castle, a chapel and hermitage, small and remote dwellings, for priests to come and pray. Anthony often went there towards the end of his life. According to Count Tiso, he saw a light in Anthony's hermitage, thought it was a fire, burst into the hermitage and saw Jesus as a child in Anthony's arms. Anthony made him promise that he would not tell this to anyone until after Anthony's death.

St. Anthony, Finder of Lost Objects: 080

Anthony died on June 13, 1231. His grave became a place where people visited and many, many miracles took place. On account of this, the bishop, clergy and nobles of Padua requested that he be canonized a saint. Less than a year after his death, Pope Gregory IX declared him a saint.

All over the world people ask St. Anthony to intercede with God so that they can find lost or stolen objects. Many pray the prayer, "Tony, Tony, turn around. Something's lost and must be found." This custom of seeking St. Anthony's help in finding lost objects goes back to an event which happened to St. Anthony himself. Anthony had a book of the Psalms which was very important to him. He had notes and comments written on it to help him when he was teaching students of his Franciscan Order. The book was precious also because it was handwritten. The Printing Press would not be invented for another 200 years. A student decided to leave the community, and took Anthony's book with him. When Anthony realized his book was missing, he prayed that it would be found or returned. After Anthony prayed the student decided to return the book and come back to the Order. The Order received him back. After Anthony's death, people began to pray to him to help them find or recover lost or stolen objects.

S.A.G. – St. Anthony Guardian of Mail: 081

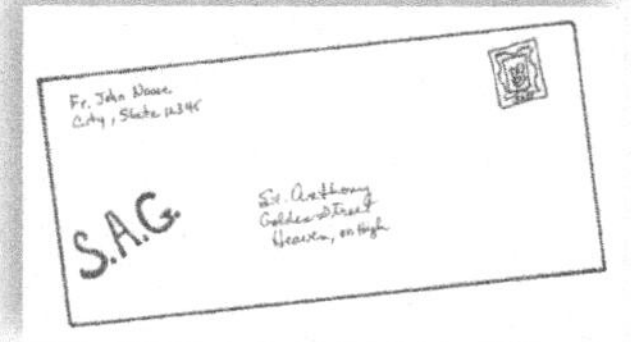

Many of us have received a letter with S.A.G. on the envelope. S.A.G. stands for St. Anthony's Guide or Guard. This custom of writing S.A.G on an envelope is said to come from an event in St. Anthony's life. He wanted to go to a place where he could rest and pray. He wrote a letter to his superior seeking permission to do so. However, when a messenger came to pick up the letter, it could not be found. Anthony took it as a sign from God that he should not go, and so he put the trip out of his mind. After a while he received a letter from his superior which was an answer to his letter telling him that he could go on the trip.

Another story connected with the mail happened in 1729. A man went from Spain to Lima, Peru. His wife remained in Spain and wrote to him on numerous occasions. There was no reply. She went to a church of St. Francis in Oviedo and placed a letter to her husband, who was in Lima, in the hand of a statue of St. Anthony. She prayed that St. Anthony would get the letter to her husband in Lima and also obtain a reply. She came to the church the next day and saw a letter in the hand of the statue of St. Anthony. She immediately began to be critical of St. Anthony for not delivering the letter. She took the letter from the statue and immediately three hundred gold coins flowed from the sleeve of the statue. On opening the letter, the wife found that it was a letter from her husband stating that when he had not received a letter from her in a long time, he thought she was dead. He said that her letter to him was delivered by a Franciscan priest.

PART THREE

EARTHLY FRIENDS

POPE – VICAR OF CHRIST

Pope:

082

The word pope comes from the Latin word papa. It is a child's word for father. The word appears in Christian literature in the writings of Tertullian (155-240 A.D.). It was a title applied to bishops indicating their spiritual fatherhood. From the 3rd to the 6th century the word was given to all bishops, but in the 7th century it began to be reserved for the Bishop of Rome, the Pope, and has been applied to him exclusively since Pope Gregory VII (1015-1085).

The Number of Popes:

The Catholic Church has a pope. The first pope was Simon Peter, the Apostle. He was appointed Pope, or visible head of the Church on earth, by Jesus Christ. There have been 266 popes, including Peter, to Pope Francis. From 217 to 1439, there have been thirty-seven antipopes. These men claimed to be pope, but in fact, were not legitimately elected, or elections were improper.

The White Cassock:

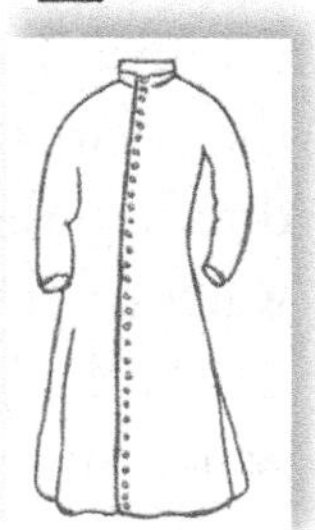

The Pope wears a white cassock. Pope Pius V (1566–1572) was a Dominican friar before he became pope. He continued to wear his coarse white Dominican habit under his papal robes. All popes, since then, have imitated this saintly Dominican by adopting white as the color of their cassocks.

Name Change:

Jesus changed the name of the first pope from Simon to Peter which means rock. Jesus said that He would build His Church upon this rock. Tradition allows popes to show esteem for a predecessor, to indicate a vision or style, or to demonstrate a total commitment to the office. Over the centuries some popes changed their name to drop a name of pagan origin. Actually, the first pope to change his name was John II in 533. His given name was Mercurius, the name of a pagan god, Mercury. Sergius IV (1009-1012) whose name was Peter di Porea, thought that it would not be proper to call himself Peter II. The last pope to keep his own name was Marcellus II in 1555. His name was Marcello Cervini.

The first pope who chose to be called by two names was Pope John Paul I. When he was elected Pope in 1978, Albino Luciani, chose the name John Paul. He took the name John because the pope who named him a bishop was St. John XXIII, and the name Paul because the pope who named him a cardinal was Pope Paul VI.

Conclave:

085

A pope is elected by the cardinals in a conclave. The word comes from two Latin words, con which is with, and clavis, which is key. So, loosely, it is a place that is locked with a key. That is what happens at a conclave. The cardinals are locked in a section of the Vatican until they elect a pope.

This custom was started by Pope Gregory X (1271-1276). It had taken the cardinals two years and nine months to elect him as Pope. The cardinals could not agree on any candidate. The local magistrate locked the electors in the episcopal palace, removed the roof subjecting the cardinals to the elements, and allowed the cardinals nothing but bread and water until they made their selection.

At the Second Council of Lyons in 1274, Pope Gregory X made rules which stated that in future elections the cardinals would be locked in until they elected a pope.

In theory, any male Catholic, even a married layman, could be elected. All popes, since Urban VI (1378), have been cardinals.

BISHOP & INSIGNIA OF OFFICE

Bishop:

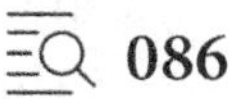
086

He is a successor of the Apostles and has the fullness of Christ's priesthood and the authority and power to administer all the Sacraments, including Ordination. There are many symbols which are connected with the bishop.

Crosier:

When the bishop celebrates Mass, he carries a staff, which is made of wood or some kind of metal. This staff is the crosier and is carried by the bishop as a symbol of his authority and of his position of giving help to the weak in faith, strengthening those losing their faith and leading back to the faith those who are going astray. Those are his duties as shepherd of the flock.

The crosier, used in Western Christianity, is a copy of the shepherd's crook, which is used for the directing of his sheep. The history of the crosier goes back to the time of the Apostles when it is said that they carried large staffs just like the travelers of their time. In the first centuries of the Church, the crosier was made of tough wood with a natural crook at the top.

In the 5th century, Pope Celestine I (422-432) stressed that the staff represented authority. It is first mentioned as a sign of the bishop's ruling power in 633 at the fourth Council of Toledo. From the 11th century, the pope did not use the crosier because his universal jurisdiction over the church was accepted. There was no need for him to use this symbol of jurisdiction.

The staff was made of the richest local woods, like cypress, ebony, or oak, and the crook at the top was made of soft metal, which was covered with gold. Sometimes gems were added. Nowadays, the crosier, made entirely of wood, is becoming popular. However, Pope Paul VI, in 1965, began to use a pastoral staff, which is somewhat like a crosier. Instead of a crook on top, there is a crucifix. Popes John Paul I, St. John Paul II and Benedict XVI also used a pastoral staff. The crosier or staff is made up of three sections so that it can be easily taken apart for storage or travel; the crook or top, the staff, and the bottom shaft.

Ring:

087

Kings and princes, when they were crowned, were given a ring as a sign of their authority to rule. The ring was worn on the fourth finger of the right hand. The kings and princes wore their ring of authority to more easily stamp official documents.

The Pope and a bishop wear a ring on the fourth finger of the right hand. The Pope's ring and the bishop's ring are a symbol of their authority and also of faith and fidelity. The bishop's ring is mentioned in 633 as part of the bishop's badge of authority. As time went on, the ring became a symbol of the bishop's marriage to the Church and his spiritual fatherhood over the faithful of his diocese.

Zucchetto:

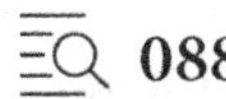

In Catholic ceremonies today, certain clerics wear a small silk cap on their head. The cap is called a zucchetto. The word comes from the Italian zuccha, a gourd or dried shell. It is a closely fitting skullcap, shaped like a saucer, and must be worn under the miter by the Pope, cardinals and bishops.

It was originally worn to protect the crown of the head from the weather. The crown of the head was bare because of the tonsure or cutting of the hair to mark one as being in the clerical state. Almost 200 years ago the zucchetto was given its present shape. Before that, it was about 3 times larger.

It is worn as an outward sign of the office held by the man wearing it. It was and is common for clothing to designate rank. We have a similar custom in the military, police, etc. Just as military officers may wear symbols to signify rank, so certain men in the church wear a zucchetto to signify their rank. In 1464 Pope Paul II granted cardinals the red zucchetto. In the 1500's the Pope reserved the white zucchetto for himself. The Pope, cardinals, and bishops are to use it by law. The Pope wears white, cardinals wear red, bishops wear magenta, which is a deep purplish red, and any cleric can wear black. The Zucchetto is like many vestments. It once had a practical purpose, and now remains part of liturgical ceremonial dress.

Biretta:

089

Cardinals, bishops and some priests wear hats that seem to be half way between a miter and a zucchetto. This hat is called a biretta. It is a square hat worn over the zucchetto. Three or four peaks rise from the top of the hat. The four-peaked hat was the academic hat of the High Middle Ages. The biretta took over 100 years to develop and by 1527, appeared as it is today.

Mitre:

090

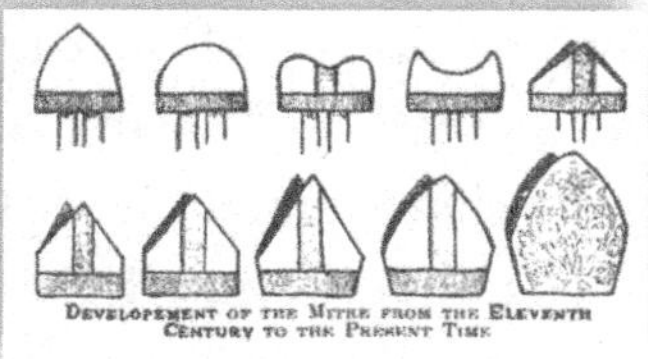

Development of the Mitre from the Eleventh Century to the Present Time

In some Catholic ceremonies, certain men wear tall hats. This type of hat, called a mitre, is a tall headdress worn by the Pope, cardinals, archbishops, bishops, and some abbots. It is used in liturgical services. Nowhere in early Christianity do we find mention of anything like the present day mitre. The shape of the modern mitre did not develop until the 11th century.

In the Western Church, the front and the back of the mitre are stiff and are shaped like upside down shields which come to a peak. These come apart when the mitre is on the head. These two pieces are sewn together at the lower part, but a hollow space separates them at the top.

In the 10th century, Pope Leo VIII is mentioned using a mitre for some non-liturgical event, and shortly afterward it became part of the dress of the Pope. In the 11th century, the mitre became a gift for bishops of special importance. The first bishop to receive the mitre was Archbishop Eberhart of Trier (1047-1066) given to him by Pope Leo IX in 1049 A.D. Before long, bishops all over Europe were depicted wearing the mitre. By the late Middle Ages and the Renaissance, bishops were always depicted in art as wearing the mitre. The mitre is the distinguishing mark of the office of bishop. It is a sign of his authority.

The two points of the hat or mitre have special meaning. They symbolize the Old and New Testaments, which the bishop is to explain to his people. The High Priest and other priests of the Old Testament wore a mitre. There are two ribbons which come down from the hat or mitre and rest on the back of the bishop. These two ribbons are called Infulae. The mitre and the infulae developed over the years.

The mitre originated in Greece before the time of Christ. It probably comes from the cap worn by athletes in Greece. The ribbons, which come from the mitre down over the back are of a more ancient origin. These ribbons were worn around the forehead, tied at the back of the head by a knot, and left to dangle down the back. During the hot summertime a soft cloth cap was placed under the bands to protect the athletes from the heat. The winners of athletic competitions were presented a laurel wreath or olive wreath, which went around the head and on the top of the cap and ribbons. This wreath marked the earliest ornamentation of the mitre. The headgear became identified as being that of a champion. This idea was copied by others, including the priests of ancient Greece and officials of the Byzantine empire. The bishop is regarded as a champion of the faith.

Pallium:

091

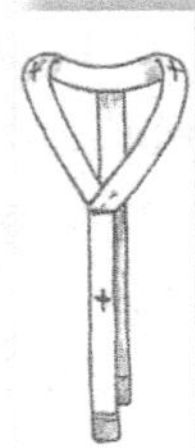

It is a narrow circular band made of white wool with two pendants about a foot long that hang from the front and the back. It is worn only by the Pope and archbishops and is a symbol of authority. From the 4th century on the feast of St. Agnes, it has been the custom to bless two lambs raised by the Trappist monks. The Latin word for lamb is agnus. The pallia are made from the wool of those lambs.

At least 400 years before Christ, the pallium was called a himation in ancient Greece and was worn in order to keep the wearer warm. The ancient himation was woolen. It was the length of the wearer plus twelve inches, and the width was a full arm's length. It was worn about the shoulders and reached the sandals, front and rear. Early Christians, clergy and lay, had adopted the himation, called a Pallium by the Romans, by the 3rd century. As time went on, it was used less and less by the laity, and eventually, the popes adopted it for themselves. By the 9th century, it was required for archbishops. Archbishops oversea larger areas than bishops.

Cross in Front of Name:

Bishops place a cross in front of their names; for example, ***+James Smith***. This custom comes from Medieval times when bishops would humbly sign their names with the title sinner or sinful servant in front of their names. The cross is a symbol of one being a sinner or one in need of the redeeming cross of Jesus Christ.

Pectoral Cross:

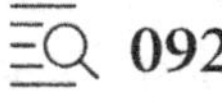 **092**

Pectoral Cross is from the Latin pectus which means bosom, breast, chest or heart. This is a cross, which is made of precious metal, sometimes decorated with jewels and suspended by a chain or cord around the neck. It is worn over the center of the chest near the heart, and its wearing was restricted to the Pope, cardinals, archbishops, bishops and abbots regardless of their attire, whether liturgical or clerical garb.

PRIEST – CALLED TO OFFER SACRIFICE

Priest:

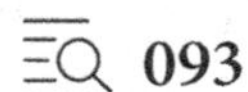 **093**

There are priests in the Catholic Church and in some other churches. What is a priest? In general, a priest is a person who is a bridge between the spiritual world and the people he represents. In ancient times, the main function of the priest was to offer sacrifice and perform ceremonies to honor the gods. Priests were to be found in ancient stable civilizations in Africa and Egypt, Asia, and the Americas. The chief priest, in many cultures, was the king. The roots of the priesthood in the Catholic Church go back over 3,000 years or 1,200 years before Christ. In Exodus 24:1-8 there is a covenant or solemn agreement between God and the Jewish people. This covenant was sealed in blood. Moses had built an altar at the foot of the mountain and twelve pillars for the twelve tribes of Israel. He sent young men to offer holocausts and to sacrifice young bulls as peace offerings to the Lord. Then Moses took half the blood and splashed it on the altar. He sprinkled the people with the other half saying, "This is the blood of the covenant which the Lord has made with you."

Jesus had His twelve Apostles with Him at the Last Supper when He said in Lk 22:20 ,"This cup is the new Covenant in my blood, which will be shed for you." This Last Supper would have reminded the Apostles and the Jews of the sacrifice and covenant spoken of in Exodus 24.

In Christianity and the New Covenant, the only priest is Jesus Christ. Jesus preached the New Covenant and sealed that New Covenant with His Blood. The Old Covenant had successors in the priesthood, but Jesus is a priest forever according to the order of Melchisedec from Hebrews 5:5-7.

In the New Testament, the word priest is used for the Jewish priesthood and is often associated with a group who opposed Jesus and His teaching from the beginning. Maybe this is the reason why the Apostles or their successors are never called priests. The term priest is used in reference to Christ in the Book of Hebrews, and also in reference to all the Christian people in 1 Peter 2:9, "You are the chosen race, a royal priesthood …". In the early part of Christ's ministry, the Twelve were sent to preach the Kingdom of God and to heal the sick in Mk 6:7-13. So, the emphasis in the New Testament is on the pastoral function of the Apostles and their successors.

Priesthood:

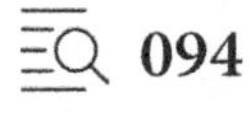

Priesthood implies sacrifice. Christ ordained the Apostles as priests at the Last Supper when He said in Lk 22:19, "Do this in remembrance of Me." The Catholic Church has always taught and understood that He commanded these Apostles and their successors in the priesthood to offer His sacrifice, the only perfect sacrifice, which is the Eucharist. The Last Supper was a sacrificial meal and not simply a religious supper. Those who were appointed to succeed the Apostles went through a rite in which hands were placed on them and a prayer was offered. This rite is referred to by St. Paul on two occasions: 1 Timothy 4:14 and 2 Timothy 1:6-8. So, this gift of God was not given directly by God, but by the imposition of hands.

The early church looked upon the priesthood as sacrificial as well as pastoral. For example, Pope Clement of Rome wrote around 95 A.D. that men piously offer the sacrifices proper to the episcopate. The sacrifices referred to were the bread and the cup. These words were used for the Eucharist or, as we now call it, The Mass. Hippolytus, who died about 235 A.D. says, "We offer the bread and the cup making Eucharist to You because You have told us to stand before You and minister as priests to You."

The connection between the New Covenant and sacrifice was seen by Christians for 1500 years until Martin Luther said that the Lord's Supper was NOT a sacrifice. He was supported in his idea by Calvin, Zwingli, and Cranmer. Luther said that the priest's function was to preach and administer the sacraments of Baptism and the Lord's Supper. The idea of sacrifice was taken away from the Lord's Supper by the Protestant leaders. The word priest is associated with sacrifice. So, the word priest was replaced in Protestant Churches by the word minister or the word pastor. Most non-Catholics say that everyone shares in the priesthood of Christ in the same way, and they quote 1 Peter 2:9, "You are a chosen race, a royal priesthood, a people set apart."

Catholics and Orthodox Christians teach that the priestly office and ministry has been given in a special way to a particular group within the Church, and this office is conferred in a special rite. This group receives special powers and graces to perform their ministry. The Catholic Church teaches that the Rite of Ordination to the Priesthood is a true and proper Sacrament, that it was instituted by Christ, that the Holy Spirit is given, and a mark is impressed on the soul. So, there are priests in the Catholic Church and Orthodox Church. Christ ordained His Apostles to be priests at the Last Supper. He wanted that priesthood to continue to offer His one perfect sacrifice to the Father. That sacrifice is the Sacrifice of the Mass.

Cassock or Soutane:

095

In the Vatican today, men are seen walking around wearing long robes. This long garment, which covers the body from neck to toe, is called cassock or soutane. It originated in France in the early 5th century. The cassock is usually called the soutane, which means beneath. This is a reference to the fact that it is worn beneath the vestments during religious services.

For the first 6 centuries of the Church, the clergy and laity wore the same type of clothing. As time went on the laity began to shorten their tunics, which was the type of clothing at that time, but the clergy maintained the longer Roman type tunics. Before the 12th century most of the people wore a heavy, long cloak lined with animal skin or fur for warmth. But by the end of the 12th century the laity used other types of clothing. The clergy continued to wear the pelisse, which was the forerunner of the cassock, because the churches were not heated. During the 12th and 13th centuries the cassock became associated entirely with the Church, and it took on the type of garment that it is today.

One of the many tasks performed by clergy in the Middle Ages was teaching, and most of the people in universities were clerics. All teachers eventually adopted the cassock as the academic gown. The secular priests who graduated from the universities simply continued to wear their black academic hats and gowns. Today's college graduates wear another variation of that dress. Centuries passed without any definite regulations. The Council of Trent (1545-63) encouraged priests to dress to conform to the priest's Order and propriety. There were no guidelines in relationship to color. Pope Sixtus V (1585-90) ordered that the cassock be used for sacred and public functions.

Men of the Cloth:

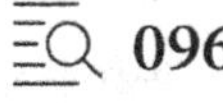

Men of the cloth today refers to clergy, but a few hundred years ago it meant anyone who wore distinctive garb, such as a military uniform made of fine broadcloth. For a while the phrase was used in relationship to professional men like doctors and lawyers, as well as clergy. Finally, the phrase is popularly used in reference to clergy.

Black Suit:

Paintings and icons of Jesus Christ, and the Apostles show them wearing different colored clothing, but seldom black. The Holy Land has a hot climate, so it is not a good place to wear heat-absorbing black. There is no special symbolic reason for wearing black. It seems that black did not take hold until the 17th century.

Until fairly recently, most Catholic clergymen wore a cassock, or habit, both of which were ankle length but not necessarily black. Franciscans wore brown, Dominicans wore white, Benedictines wore black, and so on. In 1884 the Third Council of Baltimore said that clerics were to wear the Roman collar and cassock at home and in the church, so that they could be easily recognized by the laity. The Code of Cannon Law in the 1900's states that outside of liturgical functions the priests can wear a black suit and a Roman collar.

Roman Collar:

097

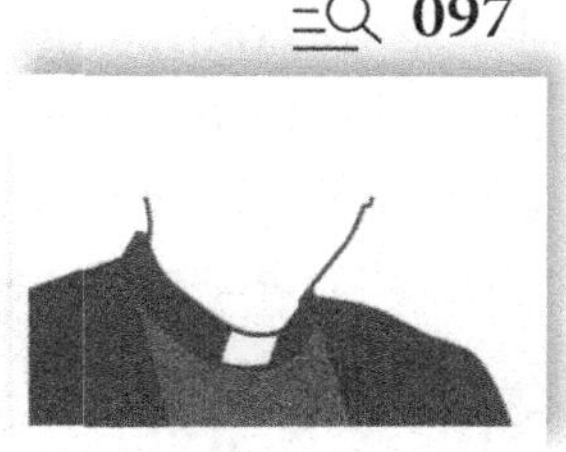

In the early Church, until about the 6th century, the priests wore the same type of clothing as everybody else. A tunic without sleeves, or toga, was worn by Roman citizens. Over this was worn a coat or cloak with sleeves, called a dalmatic. There was no such thing as a collar until the 13th century, when a narrow band began appearing at the neck of the tunic. This developed into a collar. The clerical collar originated in the 15th century when the clergy adopted the secular practice of turning the linen collar up and over their outer garment to keep it from being soiled. In paintings of the 15th to the 17th centuries, there are many different types of clerical collars. For the clergy, lace collars were not acceptable. The linen collar was stiffened and was worn mostly by the hierarchy. Diocesan priests wore a simple white cloth or scarf. In the 17th century, the collar became accepted and began to look like a primitive version of what is in use today. The Roman collar did not take its present form until the middle of the 19th century. It became the custom to attach a 3" wide starched linen collar on to the garment under the cassock. These collars became so popular that they were soon the accepted form of the clerical collar. The Roman collar is a sign of one's dedication to God.

CALLED TO SERVE

Deacon:

A permanent deacon is a married or single man who assists priests in the pastoral and administrative care of souls. There is also the transitional deacon who is ordained to the diaconate but who ultimately will be ordained to the priesthood.

CALLED TO HOLINESS

Religious Orders:

These are communities of men and women who serve the Church. Some profess solemn vows of poverty, chastity and obedience. Some make a profession to their particular Rule of Life. The communities have various charisms and apostolates.

Nun & Sister:

A nun is a woman who belongs to a religious order with solemn vows of poverty, chastity and obedience and lives in a cloistered monastic life. A sister is a woman who belongs to a religious order with simple vows or public vows not recognized by the Church as solemn.

Brother:

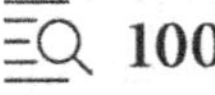

Brothers are religious men who are not ordained to the priesthood. They take vows of poverty, chastity and obedience. They live together and share their possessions.

Monk:

A monk is a man who leaves society in order to live a life totally dedicated to God. He lives in a community of men in a monastery, abbey or priory. Monks take vows of poverty, chastity and obedience, and live according to a specific rule, such as the Rule of St. Benedict.

Hermit: 101

A hermit is a person who lives alone away from society in order to devote himself or herself to prayer and to the interior life. A hermit can live anonymously without a public commitment. The local bishop usually requires a rule of life written by the hermit. This image is St. Paul of Thebes, the first hermit.

Third Orders: 102

A Third Order is a group of lay people connected to consecrated religious and who follow a particular rule and spirituality. Today, the most famous of these Third Orders are the Franciscans, Dominicans and Carmelites.

Consecrated Life:

Some men and women feel called to the consecrated life which is modeled on the life of Jesus Christ and, even more deeply, on the mystery of the Holy Trinity. The core of consecrated life is selfless love. The Three Persons of the Trinity are united by their infinite love. Jesus Christ is the Incarnation of this Divine Love. The men and woman who consecrate themselves do so by following in the footsteps of Jesus and thus reflect on earth the total self-giving which is at the heart of Christianity.

Laity: 103

Those who have received Baptism but who are not in priesthood or in a religious state of life which has been approved by the Church.

PART FOUR

THE PUBLIC WORSHIP OF THE CHURCH

LITURGY

Liturgy: 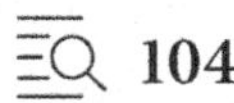 104

Liturgy is the public worship of the Church, the Church being the people of God, and includes the rites and ceremonies of the Mass, Sacraments, and the Liturgy of the Hours. In the Liturgy, we use lots of words and gestures. When people come together in the presence of their God and speak with Him, it is natural that they use some bodily positions and gestures to express their reverence.

Words and gestures are parts of human language. Words appeal to the hearing, and gestures appeal to the sight. Hearing and seeing are the two senses closest to the intellect and therefore, closest to the spiritual life. Words and gestures work together to give a powerful message.

All religions use rites or ways of conducting ceremonies which can be seen or heard in order to strengthen and communicate the desires of the soul. Christian prayer wants the human body to be involved because Jesus Christ, the Son of God, took on a human body. When people use bodily gestures in prayer, they are simply doing what Jesus Christ Himself did in prayer. He lifted His eyes to heaven, prostrated Himself, etc. He used gestures as a way to perform miracles when just one word would have been enough. He taught by gestures when He washed His disciples' feet. He offered His Body on the Cross in the perfect act of worship. Special meaning is given to the gestures used in the Prayer of the Liturgy.

There is a great deal of movement during the Liturgy and at other times. We will find that these gestures were practiced in the Bible and have a great deal of meaning. In this section, we will explain the Liturgy first and then the gestures carried out in the Liturgy; for example, standing, kneeling, etc., and we will also explain the vessels and finally the vestments used in the Liturgy.

Mass: 105

The Mass is the principal celebration of the Church's public worship and is an unbloody re-presentation of Jesus' sacrifice and a meal with words from the Last Supper. The first part of the Mass, called the Liturgy of the Word, contains Scripture readings and prayers. The second part is the Liturgy of the Eucharist. St. John Paul the Great said the Eucharist is the source and summit of the Catholic Church. The bread and wine are changed into the Body, Blood, Soul and Divinity of Jesus Christ. This is called transubstantiation.

Wheat, Grapes, Chalice, and Host: 106

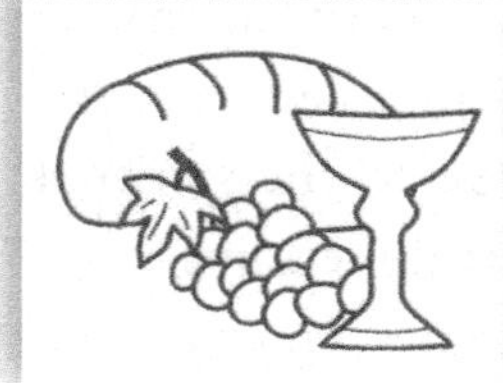

The Church uses the wheat and grapes to remind us of the bread and wine consumed at the Last Supper, the sacrifice of the Mass. In the first sacrifice of the Mass, the chalice is used to contain the wine, and the host is the bread. The wine and the bread are our gifts offered to God.

The bread and wine are not mere symbols, but at the words of Consecration, they become the Body, Blood, Soul and Divinity of Jesus Christ, which is a promise of eternal life.

Loaves & Fishes: 107

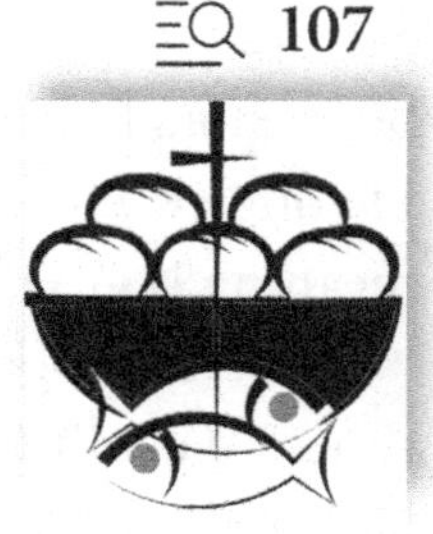

Jesus performed the miracle of multiplying the loaves and the fishes. The loaves and fishes are used as a symbol. Together they are a symbol of the Eucharist and are to be found in the catacombs in Rome. This was where the early Christians often celebrated Mass, or the Eucharistic Sacrifice, during which the bread and wine are changed into the Body, Blood, Soul and Divinity of Jesus Christ. The early Christians guarded the Eucharistic Sacrifice zealously. Those entering the Church community had to study the teaching of the Church for a long time and had to prove themselves to be trustworthy in those times of persecution. So, this is why the symbol of the loaves and fishes was and is used to designate the Eucharistic feast.

Bread & Wine:

108

Bread and wine are offered at the Mass because Jesus offered bread and wine at the Last Supper, which was the first Mass. Then, He told His Apostles, "Do this in memory of me." Why would Jesus Christ choose those two particular substances? We can give a guess as to why He chose them. Bread and wine have to go through tremendous suffering in order to become what they end up as being. First of all, the bread comes from wheat, which must pass through the harshness of winter, be ground in a mill, and finally be put through fire as it is being baked into bread. The wine comes from grapes. These grapes go through the winepress where the life is crushed out of them in order to produce wine. These two substances symbolize the suffering and death of Jesus Christ in order for us to get to heaven.

Bread and wine clearly symbolize unity. The bread is made from many, many grains of wheat, and wine is made from lots of grapes. Many people become one in Jesus Christ. In Jn 17:20-21, Jesus prayed, "Father, that they may be one as we are one. That they may be one in us." Bread and wine have always fed man. When we consume bread and wine, they become part of us. When we bring bread and wine to the altar to be offered to God, we bring ourselves to be offered. Jesus took bread and wine and changed them into Himself. Then, He gives Himself to us in the Eucharist under the appearance of bread and wine. He gives us His Flesh to eat and His Blood to drink in order to feed us spiritually (see John Chapter 6).

Kind of Bread:

109

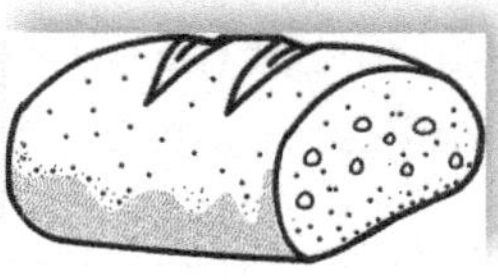

Jesus Christ instituted the Eucharist. Bread is one of the two necessary elements of the Eucharist. Wine is the other element. The Eastern Churches, for the most part, make use of leavened bread, bread made with yeast, while the Western Church, since early times, has used both leavened and unleavened bread. Only bread made of wheat is recognized by the Catholic Church as a valid element for the Mass. In the beginning, the faithful took bread from their supply at home and brought it for the Mass. Consequently, the Eucharistic bread did not differ from the shape of bread used in homes.

As time went on, the altar breads assumed a round form of moderate thickness in the Western Church. A growing reverence for the Eucharist effected a change so that altar breads were specially prepared. The 1983 Code of Canon Law 926 set down the present-day requirements for unleavened altar breads.

Host:

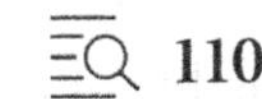 **110**

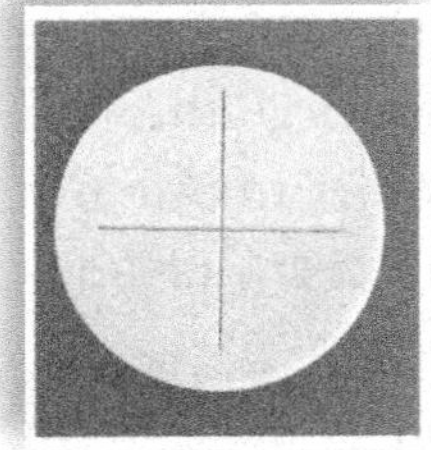

Holy Communion is called a Host. The word host comes from the Latin word hostia, which is an animal slain in sacrifice. In Holy Communion, we receive the Body, Blood, Soul and Divinity of Jesus Christ, Who was slain in sacrifice for our sins. Catholics use small round hosts for Holy Communion. Only flour and water may be used in baking bread for the Eucharist. It is not legal to add other ingredients.

The Jews were obliged to use unleavened bread, bread without yeast, for the Passover meal. This was done in memory of the time when they were escaping from Egypt, with Moses leading them, and they did not have time to wait for their daily-baked bread to rise. Jesus used this kind of bread at the Last Supper.

Pictures drawn in the first century of Christianity in the catacombs in Rome show the bread to be round. A mold or baking iron for making round, flat hosts was found in Carthage in North Africa. It dates from the 6th or 7th century which was before the Muslims conquered that region in 698. The wafer thinness of the bread comes from at least the middle of the 11th century. The hosts have to be thin because, if they are thick, the outside would be baked but not the inside. The coin-size of our modern altar breads dates from the 20th century. Initially, they were cut by hand using cookie cutters. Then, machinery was invented to produce the hosts.

Holy Communion on the Tongue: 111

Some Catholics receive Communion on the tongue, and others receive in the hand. During the first few centuries of Christianity, Holy Communion was received in the hand. However, the teaching on the Eucharist developed. Also abuses in connection with the Eucharist increased, such as taking the Host home for satanic rites or trying to work magic with It.

The Church gradually insisted that the Holy Communion be received on the tongue. The Councils of Saragossa in 380 and Toledo in the 5th to 7th centuries established the law to receive Communion on the tongue, and this has been confirmed by later councils. It is still the practice for the churches of the East, both Catholic and Orthodox. In the 11th century, Eucharistic regulations were devised to control every aspect of the Eucharist.

During the Protestant Revolt the issue of Holy Communion in the hand came up. For those protesting, it was a way of asserting the priesthood of the laity and also of denying the Real Presence of Jesus Christ in the Eucharist. The Catholic Church continued to require people to receive Holy Communion on the tongue. In the 1960's, some countries, like Holland, France, and Canada, began to experiment with receiving Holy Communion in the hand. In 1969, Pope Paul VI gave many good reasons as to why receiving Holy Communion in the hand was not a good practice, and also that to receive Holy Communion on the tongue was to be preferred and kept. However, he said that if two-thirds of the bishops in a country asked Rome for permission to give Holy Communion in the hand, the permission would be given. The Bishops of the United States sought and on June 17, 1977 received permission to distribute Communion in the hand.

Language:

112

Today, the Mass is offered in the language of the people. It was not always that way. The Mass was offered in Latin for hundreds of years. The first Mass was offered by Jesus at the Last Supper almost certainly in Aramaic. It was the language spoken by Jesus, the Apostles and first converts. Aramaic was the common language of Palestine in New Testament times, and the writers of the Gospels used Aramaic phrases like "Talitha, koum", "Little girl I say to you arise", in Mk 5:41, and "Eli, Eli, lema sabachthani", "My God, My God why have You forsaken Me", in Mt 27:46.

Probably, Jesus also spoke Hebrew because He read from the Prophet Isaiah in the synagogue (see Lk 4:16-21). The Book of Isaiah was written in Hebrew, which was the language of the Old Testament and which was used in the Temple. There is no evidence that the early Christians tried to use Hebrew. Greek was popular in urban areas and was the next language of the Liturgy or the language used in the Mass. Rome laid aside Greek in favor of Latin somewhere in the 3rd and 4th centuries. The person most responsible for this was Pope Damasus I (366-384). Latin was the language of cultured people and was the obvious language for Church meetings because people came to those meetings from all over the known world. Throughout the centuries other cultures joined the gatherings. They spoke different languages, but gradually accepted Latin. The Church in the West used Latin in the Liturgy for about the next 1600 years until Vatican II allowed the Mass to be said in the language of the people while maintaining the rich Latin language as the official language of the Church. There is some Greek in the Mass today. It is the "Kyrie Eleison", which means, "Lord, Have Mercy". It was ordered to be sung by Pope St. Gelasius I (492-496).

Raising of Host & Chalice:

113

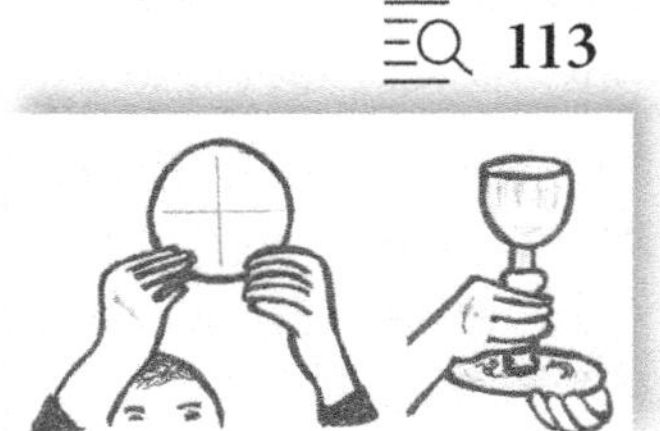

The Priest raises up the Host and chalice after the Consecration. He does this so that the people can see and adore Jesus Christ. In the 11th century, Berengarius of Tours denied the fact that Jesus Christ is really present in the Eucharist. The reaction of the people to this was that they wanted to see the Host which had just been changed into the Body of Christ, and they wanted to adore Him. In the 1200's the Archbishop of Paris, Eudes de Sully, instructed his priests to hold up the Host after the Consecration. The gesture spread rapidly through France, England and Germany, and within 50 years was in all churches in the West. People were continually encouraged to look up at the Host and adore Jesus. This is true even today when people are encouraged to look at the Host and say something like, "My Jesus, I adore You."

The raising up of the chalice was not in common use until the 14th century. The people could not see the Precious Blood in the chalice, so their desire was not as pressing as their desire to see the Host. The raising of the chalice was put in as a required part of Mass in the missal of Pope Pius V in 1570.

Where First Celebrated? 114

The Masses were celebrated in the time of the Apostles and for the first 300 years in the homes of the people on the family table. They had to gather in secret because of the persecutions.

Obligation: 115

Catholics are required to attend Mass on Sundays and Holy Days. During the first 300 years of Christianity people were intermittently persecuted, and so there was no ruling that one had to attend Mass. Attending Mass became obligatory in the 6th century through a decree of the Council of Agde. All Catholics, 7 years and older, who had reached the age of reason, were obliged to attend Sunday Mass. This later became universal law in the 1917 Code of Canon Law 1247 and 1248 and affirmed in the 1983 Code of Canon Law.

This is based on the 3rd Commandment to "Remember to keep holy the Sabbath Day," found in Ex 20:8. Also, it was based on the fact that

Jesus rose from the dead on Sunday, and the Holy Spirit came upon the Apostles on Sunday.

Book of the Gospels:

116

The *Book of the Gospels* is carried into Church before Mass and the priest kisses it at Mass. The Catholic Church venerates the Scriptures and shows many signs of reverence for the Word of God, especially in the Liturgy. The *Book of Gospels* is carried in solemn procession before Mass, and two candles are carried ahead of it. Before the Gospel is read at Mass, to show reverence for the Gospel, the priest or deacon may incense the book. The book is kissed after the Gospel is read, another sign of reverence for the Word of God.

Catholics do not support the idea that the Bible is self-explanatory. It requires the community that formed the Bible to interpret it. The Catholic Church took almost 400 years to put the Bible together. It sifted through almost forty Gospels and decided that only four of those Gospels were inspired and worthy of being included in the Bible. The Catholic Church examined at least seven books of Revelation and decided that only one was inspired. The Catholic Church decided that only one of at least sixteen Acts was inspired and gave us the Acts of the Apostles.

There were many books in existence in the early Catholic Church and the Church declared that only twenty-seven of those books were inspired. These twenty-seven books make up the New Testament. We must remember that the Catholic Church wrote the New Testament and preserved the entire Bible by having monks write it by hand from about 400 A.D. until the invention and use of the printing press in 1450.

Until the printing press, the people did not have a Bible because they were handwritten, expensive and few people could read. There were Bibles in libraries and Bibles chained to pulpits, just like phone books used to be chained to the walls, so that they would be available to the people and could not be stolen.

The Catholic Church cherishes and reverences the Bible as is indicated by the carrying of the *Book of Gospels* in procession at the beginning of Mass and by the kissing of the book after the Gospel has been read.

Roman Missal:

117

In the Extraordinary Rite of the Mass, a large book is used. The book is called the Roman Missal and contains the complete text of the Mass of the Roman Rite for every day of the year. The Scripture readings, prayers and Order of the Mass are contained in it. From the beginning of Christianity, the Mass was composed of readings from the Scriptures, prayers and the Thanksgiving Prayer or Eucharistic Prayer, which contained the account of Jesus' institution of the Eucharist and the Commemoration of His Passion, death and Resurrection.

At first, the prayers were not written down. Later on, different forms of prayer were written down, but there was no book which contained the whole text of the Mass. The Scripture readings were read from the Bible. Sometime later, a special Lectionary was put together. The prayers and Eucharistic Prayers were in a book call the Sacramentary. Over the years these books were joined together into one book, which was called the Missal.

The word missal was used in France and England in the 8th century. Some churches, to save money, tied the Lectionary and Sacramentary together. In the 13th century, Missals gradually took over because of low Masses in which the celebrant took the parts of other ministers and choir. But there still was no uniformity. The Council of Trent set about a reform of the Liturgy, and Pope St. Pius V, in 1570, ordered the reform, which was gradually accepted everywhere. There were very few reforms in the Liturgy from 1570 until the 2nd Vatican Council (1962-65) and the reform of Pope Paul VI in 1969 and 1975. There have been eight editions of the Roman Missal from 1604 to 2002.

Low Mass:

A Low Mass is a Mass said by the priest with few people attending. This contrasts with a High Mass which the priest said with some other clerics helping him and possibly singing some parts of the Mass.

Tridentine Mass:

118

Tridentine Mass, so called because it is a result of the reforms of the Council of Trent (1545), is the Mass issued by Pope Pius V (1566-1572). The Mass is in Latin.

The Liturgy of the Hours:

119

It is the common prayer of the Church for everyone. It is a simple way to pray, and one can pray it alone or with a group. With the Liturgy of the Hours, people can pray the Psalms, read the Scripture, and pray with the whole Church. It is also known as the Breviary or the Divine Office, and is part of the Liturgy of the Church or official prayer of the Church. It is prayed all over the world by the Church. From ancient tradition the prayer consecrates the course of the day and night with five different periods of prayer called hours. A person can pray it all at one time of the day or can combine some of the hours depending on their schedule.

The format consists of an opening prayer, a hymn, praying Psalms, a reading from Scripture, praying for others, the *Our Father*, and a concluding prayer. If prayed by oneself, the Morning and Evening Prayer take 10 minutes each, and if prayed with others, take 15 to 20 minutes. The custom of gathering at certain times of the day to pray was practiced before Christianity began. The early Christians prayed together at certain hours. The Rosary was popular with the laity, while the monks prayed the Liturgy of the Hours. Today, the Morning Prayer and/or Evening Prayer are prayed by groups in some parishes and by people in consecrated life. Many lay people pray the Liturgy of the Hours in their own homes.

Music:

The music mostly used in Catholic worship until recently was Gregorian Chant. This form of chant was first made popular by Pope St. Gregory the Great (540-604).

Consecrations:

The Catholic Church refers to consecrations of persons, places and things. Consecration is the setting apart of any person, place or thing for the service of God. A person can consecrate oneself to God in an informal way by saying the Morning Offering of the Apostleship of Prayer each morning.

O Jesus, through the Immaculate Heart of Mary, I offer Thee my prayers, works, and sufferings of this day for all the intentions of Thy Sacred Heart, in union with the Holy Sacrifice of the Mass throughout the world, in reparation for my sins, for the intentions of all our associates, and in particular for the intention recommended this month by the Holy Father. Amen.

ADORATION

Adoration of the Blessed Sacrament:

120

Adoration is the homage paid to the Blessed Sacrament exposed on the altar or reserved in the tabernacle. St. John Paul II explains that the Eucharist is the source and summit of the Christian life. At Mass the bread and wine are changed into the Body, Blood, Soul and Divinity of Jesus Christ, and is given to the people, or is preserved. In the early centuries of the Church, some of the consecrated Hosts were kept in a container called a ciborium or pyx and given to the sick.

The first eleven or twelve centuries of Church history reveal only traces of these devotions of Adoration of the Blessed Sacrament. Four types of devotion emerged in connection with the reserved Blessed Sacrament: they are Procession, Eucharistic Congresses, Perpetual and Forty Hours Exposition, and Benediction.

Processions:

Processions began when the Eucharist was being moved from one place to another. People began to walk together behind the Eucharist. These processions gradually became a regular practice when Pope Urban IV established the Feast of Corpus Christi, or the Body of Christ, for the entire Church in 1264. Every procession is a sign of the pilgrim Church, the body of those who believe in Christ, on their way to Heaven.

Eucharistic Congresses:

121

Eucharistic Congresses are meetings for clergy and laity for the purpose of gaining a better understanding of, and greater devotion to, the Holy Eucharist. They began in 1881 in Lille, France. There have been 50 Eucharistic Congresses since then. The last was in Dublin, Ireland, in 2012. They may be local, national or international and have been held all over the world. Two have been in the United States. The 28th Eucharistic Congress was held in Chicago in 1926 and the 41th was held in Philadelphia in 1976.

Exposition:

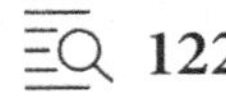

The Albigensian heresy spread in France in the 12th century. The first recorded instance of Perpetual Adoration or continuous Adoration came about when King Louis VIII defeated the Albigensians in September 1226. He called on the people to thank Jesus in the Blessed Sacrament exposed in the Chapel of the Holy Cross at Avignon, France. So many people came to adore that the Bishop decided to let Adoration continue without end. Rome agreed with his decision, and Adoration continued without interruption for the next 566 years from 1226 until the persecutions of the French Revolution in 1792. It resumed in 1829.

Exposition of the Blessed Sacrament began first in tabernacles, then with the tabernacle doors opened. Finally in the Middle Ages, the Blessed Sacrament was exposed in a monstrance, a tall decorated sacred vessel. This spread over Europe and came to a high point with the establishment of the Feast of Corpus Christi by Pope Urban IV in 1264. The followers of St. Norbert and the Eucharistic hymns of St. Thomas Aquinas were instrumental in bringing this about.

Perpetual Adoration or continuous Adoration of the Blessed Sacrament, 24 hours a day 7 days a week, became popular in the beginning of the 16th century. It was declared by the Council of Trent and approved by Pope Julius in 1551. This time marked the beginning of the Protestant Movement when churches were looted and the Blessed Sacrament desecrated. Faithful Catholics made reparation to Jesus by staying in His Presence in Adoration around the clock. The 40 Hours Exposition began in Milan in the middle of the 1500's and was formally recognized by Pope Clement VIII in 1592. In the 19th century, 40 Hour Exposition was begun in Philadelphia, PA by St. John Neumann and continues in many churches today.

Benediction: 123

Benediction consists of exposing the Sacred Host in a monstrance which is placed on the altar and incensed. Prayers are said, hymns are sung, and the priest blesses the people with the Sacred Host which is visible in the monstrance. The custom probably came about from the showing of the Host at different stopping places during the Corpus Christi Procession in the 13th century. The first example of Benediction as we have it today was at Hildesheim, Germany in the 15th century. It came as a response to the peoples' desire to look upon the Host after the Consecration.

BLESSINGS

Blessings: 124

In the Bible the word blessed is used over and over again. To bless means to call down God's care on some person, place or thing. In the Old Testament, the emphasis is on the fact that all blessings come from the Lord, and the Lord gives His blessing freely to whomever He chooses. It was common for people to greet one another by a prayer for blessing from the Lord.

In Old Testament times, some people had special authority to call down God's blessing upon others. A father has special authority to call down God's blessing upon his children, a king upon his people, and priests upon the people. The Israelites did not believe that they could give more power to the Lord by blessing Him. For them, to bless meant to give thanks or to give praise.

In the New Testament, there is a two-pronged meaning to blessing: First, the calling down of God's generosity upon people; Second, thanks given to God. An example of this is Luke 24:51-53 where Jesus ascends to His Father as He blesses His disciples, and His disciples go back to Jerusalem praising and blessing God.

This idea of calling down God's blessing and giving thanks to God is to be found in the Eucharist or Mass. At the Last Supper, the blessing of Jesus Christ was a prayer of thanksgiving to the Father, and also a calling down of the Father's power to make something holy (in Luke 24:30 & Mt. 26:26).

The early Christians gave blessings. Early Christian writers, like Hippolytus and Serapion, tell us about the blessings of water, honey, milk, lights and oil for the sick. These blessings were given during the Mass. Why? Probably to show the relationship of these blessings to the greatest of all the blessings that God has given to us, and that blessing is Jesus Christ, His own Son and His work of redeeming us.

The Bible is full of examples of giving and receiving blessings. In the Catholic Church, we have a *Book of Blessings* which has almost 900 pages. The *Catechism of the Catholic Church* states that every baptized person is called upon to be a blessing and to bless (CCC 1669). At Baptism the parents and godparents are invited to bless the baby by making the sign of the cross on the baby's forehead.

Priests are often asked to bless persons, places or things which dedicates them to a sacred purpose, or a spiritual value is attached to them. God uses the things of this world to speak to us in order to strengthen our faith, so we should not tune those things out. There are many, many things made to work on our senses and turn our minds and hearts to God. Some of these things are: Rosaries, medals, pictures, stained-glass windows, incense, statues, flowers, etc.

Why do people say, "God bless you," when someone sneezes?

There are varying accounts as to the origin of this prayer. One belief is that it originated in Rome when the bubonic plague was raging through Europe. One of the symptoms of the plague was coughing and sneezing. It is believed that Pope Gregory I (Gregory the Great) suggested saying, "God bless you" after a person sneezed in hopes that this prayer would protect the person from an otherwise certain death.

The expression may have also originated from superstition. Some people believe that the custom of asking for God's blessing began when ancient man thought that the soul was in the form of air and resided in the body's head. A sneeze, therefore, might accidentally expel the spirit from the body unless God blessed that person and prevented this from occurring. Some ancient cultures also thought that sneezing forced evil spirits out of the body endangering others because these spirits might now enter their bodies. The blessing was bestowed to protect both the person who sneezed and others around him or her (from *Library of Congress*).

Whatever its origin, it is a beautiful prayer.

Imposition of Hands: 125

This is an ancient symbol which the Catholic Church adopted from the time of the Apostles. It signifies the giving of a blessing, power or consecration. In the Old Testament, it had a sacrificial meaning and also imparted a blessing. In the New Testament, Jesus imposed hands to heal the sick. The Apostles imposed hands to give authority and powers, and soon it was the accepted means of ordaining and conferring office. In the ceremony of the ordination of a priest, the bishop ordains a man to the priesthood through the laying on of hands. In the Anointing of the Sick, the priest lays his hands on the sick person. In the Sacrament of Reconciliation, the priest raises his right hand when giving absolution. And at Mass, the priest places his hands over the gifts on the altar.

GESTURES

Sign of the Cross:

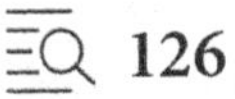 **126**

One of the most common ways to recognize a Catholic is when a person is seen making the sign of the cross. How is it made properly and what is said while making it? “In the name of the Father, and of the Son, and of the Holy Spirit. Amen”.

Catholics grow up making the sign of the cross. It is second nature to us. It is a way we recognize another Catholic. We place our left hand on our chest, and we move our right hand to our forehead as we say, “In the name of the Father”; then we move our right hand to our chest as we say, “and of the Son”; and as we move our right hand from the left to the right shoulder we say, “and of the Holy Spirit”. Then we join our hands together as we say, “Amen”. We begin and end our prayers with the sign of the cross.

The sign of the cross began at Calvary when Christ first made it by hanging on the cross. The early Christians often traced a small cross on their foreheads, and it was for them, as it is for us today, a sign of faith. Fathers and mothers are encouraged to make the sign of the cross over their children. Tracing the sign of the cross over a person or object as a blessing did not come into use until the Middle Ages. It replaced the more traditional laying on of hands. The custom of signing oneself with Holy Water when entering or leaving the Church is a reminder of our Baptism and a symbol of the renewal of our baptismal promises. If made properly and meaningfully, this gesture can extend into every part of our lives; for example, before starting any difficult work, before starting a journey, before and after meals. The value depends on the love and meaning we consciously put into it. The more slowly and deliberately we make the sign of the cross, the more likely it will affect our lives.

Sign of the Cross – History

The early Christians have left us many things. One of these things is the sign of the cross. It identified them as followers of Christ, just as it does for us today. They were persecuted greatly and had to hide the fact that they were Christians. They used to identify themselves by tracing a cross on the ground with a stick or their sandal, and then quickly wipe it out.

Tracing a cross on the forehead became popular almost from the beginning of Christianity. Tertullian, who died about 240 A. D. said, "In all our actions, when we come in or go out, when we dress, we wash, at our meals, before resting to sleep, we make on our forehead the sign of the cross. These practices are not committed by a formal law of Scripture, but tradition teaches them, custom confirms them, and faith observes them." St. Cyril of Jerusalem, who died around 386 A.D. said, "Let us not be ashamed to confess the Crucified. Be the cross our seal, made with boldness by our fingers and on our brow and in everything: over the bread we eat, and the cups we drink; in our comings in and in our goings out; before we sleep, when we lie down and when we awake; when we are traveling, and when we are at rest. Make it on your forehead so that devils, at sight of the standard of the King, may flee away trembling." St. Jerome, who died in 420 A.D. said that the sign of the cross was sometimes made on the lips. Prudentius, a Christian poet who died in 405 A.D., mentioned that the sign was made on the chest.

The small sign of the cross was commonly used by the end of the 4th century. In the 5th and 6th centuries, a heresy or false teaching, called the Monophysite Heresy, spread. It taught that Christ had only one Nature. The Christians, who believed what the Apostles had taught, wanted to emphasize that Christ had two Natures, His divine Nature and His human Nature. It was suggested that people make a large cross with two fingers signifying the two Natures of Christ. That custom is observed even today when the Pope gives his blessing, with two fingers extended.

In different places, during the following years, the sign of the cross was made with three fingers extended, in honor of the Blessed Trinity, Three Persons in One God. The other two fingers were bent to the palm of the hand to signify that Christ had two Natures, a human Nature and a divine Nature.

At Mass, the sign of the cross was made in any of three ways:

With three fingers – in honor of the Blessed Trinity;

With one finger – in honor of the Oneness of God;

With five fingers extended, as we do today – in honor of the five wounds of Christ.

In the 13th century, Pope Innocent III decreed that the sign of the cross should be made with three fingers from the forehead to the chest, and from the right to the left shoulder. At a later date, the whole hand was used, and the direction changed from the left to the right shoulder. Even today, in the Byzantine Rite, which is joined to the Catholic Church, they touch the thumb and first two fingers together and move from the forehead, to the chest, to the right, and then to the left shoulder. All other Catholics join their five fingers and touch their forehead, chest, left shoulder, and right shoulder.

While one is making this sign, the words used have differed over the years. Some of the older prayers were: "In the Name of the Holy Trinity"; "In the Name of Jesus of Nazareth"; and so on.

Sign of the Cross – Meaning:

The sign of the cross sums up the teaching of Christ, and especially brings out to us the fact that there are three Persons in One God, the Blessed Trinity, and the fact that Christ died on the cross for us. We say, "In the Name," not "names." By saying this we proclaim our faith in One God. When we say, "Of the Father, and of the Son, and of the Holy Spirit", we proclaim our belief in the Blessed Trinity or three Persons in One God. When we make the sign of the cross itself, we proclaim our belief in Our Lord having become a man and that He died and rose from the dead. These are the basic teachings of our faith.

We make the sign of the cross as we pass in front of the Catholic Church to indicate our belief that Jesus is really present in the Blessed Sacrament, and we want to honor Him. We make the sign of the cross when we get up, at work, at play, before and after meals, and as often as we can. It reminds us of the Father, Son and Holy Spirit, and the fact that Jesus died on the cross for us. The sign of the cross can help us in the times of temptation. The book, *The Imitation of Christ* says, that if you confide in the Lord, strength will be given you from heaven, and the world and the flesh shall be made subject to you. Neither will you fear your enemy, the devil, if you be armed with faith and signed with the Cross of Christ.

St. Hippolytus, who lived in the 3rd century, said, "When tempted, always reverently seal your forehead with the sign of the cross. This sign of the Passion is displayed and made manifest against the devil if you make it in faith, not in order that you may be seen by men, but by putting it forward like a shield."

Shepherds put a mark on their sheep to show that they own these sheep. When soldiers were recruited into a particular general's army, there was a mark tattooed on their hands to show that they belonged to that general. Also, slaves were branded with the sign of their owner. When a person was sealed with the sign of the cross at Baptism, he or she understood that they were acknowledging that Jesus Christ is owner of their lives. Whenever that person made the sign of the cross, it meant that he or she was once more declaring that they belonged to Christ. We bear the mark of Our Lord and Master.

The sign of the cross is made while all of the Seven Sacraments are being given to remind us that the graces given in these sacraments come from Christ's death and Resurrection. The sign of the cross is made during the Mass, when a priest gives his blessing, in times of temptation, etc. From the beginning of Christianity, the sign of the cross was a badge of identification, a shield in times of temptation, a demonstration of belief in the Blessed Trinity and Christ's death on the cross.

Sign of the Cross – Gospel:

Before the priest or deacon reads the Gospel at Mass, he makes the sign of the cross on his forehead, on his lips, and on his chest. The sign of the cross on the forehead indicates that we believe in the good news of the Gospel. The sign of the cross on the lips indicates that we must preach the Gospel by word of mouth. And the sign of the cross on the chest indicates that we must treasure the Word of God in our hearts.

Fr. Almire Pichon, a Jesuit priest and spiritual director for St. Terese of Lisieux, once said, "I believed that if our signs of the cross were always made as if in the presence of God, rather than if we were chasing away flies, they would open for us the heart of God. Each sign of the cross brings us nearer to God. For each sign of the cross well made, there is one added degree of eternal glory. Each sign of the cross made with devotion deposits within your heart another degree of love, which you would not have had without it."

Sign of the Cross and Kiss Hands:

Some people kiss their hands after making the sign of the cross. They are really kissing the cross they form with the forefinger and thumb at right angles after the larger cross has been made.

The form of the cross made by the thumb and forefinger symbolized the cross of our redemption. The three fingers left standing straight together symbolize the Trinity. While using these two symbols, they pray:

> (Making a small cross on the forehead, say) "By the Sign of the Cross,
> (Making a small cross on the lips, say) from our enemies deliver us, O Lord,
> (Making a small cross on the chest, say) in the Name of the Father, and of the Son and of the Holy Spirit.
> (Making the sign of the cross in the usual way, say) Amen."
> (End by kissing the fingers that made the sign of the cross.)

Prostration:

127

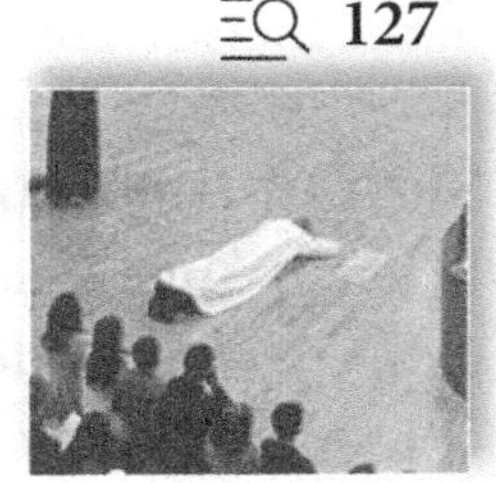

Prostration, or to lie flat, face down, on the ground or floor, in adoration or submission is sometimes practiced. It is in the Liturgy on Good Friday and in the ordination ceremony of a deacon, priest or bishop. This is a more total way of expressing the same sentiments shown in genuflection; that is, adoration, penance and begging. It was common among ancient people, especially the Jews. It is in the New Testament in Mt. 17:6; 26:39. It was fairly common in the early Church and means that we are submitting ourselves totally to God.

Bow:

It is a gesture that is somewhere between standing and genuflecting. It is a humble way of adoring God, and it is also a way of showing reverence, respect, gratitude and veneration towards people or objects. Bowing was a common gesture in pagan rites and originally came from oriental courts to the courts of the Roman Empire. It was introduced into early Christian prayer and became one of the most commonly used gestures in the Liturgy. It is used to express reverence for saints, sacred objects, high ranking ministers of God like bishops, the altar and a crucifix. The Church in the East has the custom of bowing instead of genuflecting.

Eyes Raised:

It was always believed that God had His dwelling above the sky. People want their soul to communicate with God. They join this desire with two bodily gestures using the eyes and the hands. These gestures were common among the pagans and the Jews. They were used by Christ Himself (Jn. 11:41) and also by His followers. When we raise our eyes this indicates that we are fixing our full attention, placing our confidence in, and turning our whole being toward God.

Orans:

128

Orans is from Medieval Latin translated as one who is praying. Orans is a posture with the elbows close to the sides of the body and with the hands outstretched sideways, palms up. Drawings are found often in the Roman catacombs. These figures may be of a person of great dignity clothed in a large garment which comes down to the feet. The person's arms and hands are extended in the ancient posture of prayer. This is the posture that the priest uses during the Eucharistic Prayer and other parts of the Mass. The orans is usually a feminine figure and is a symbol of the praying Church, of the soul, or of Our Lady.

Hands Raised:

The tongue is the most effective instrument to communicate the thoughts of the soul. The hands are the next most effective. The Liturgy tries to make full use of them. Our custom today is to join our hands in prayer. A more ancient custom was the raising and extending the hands, along with standing erect. This posture was taken to represent the posture of Christ on the cross when He offered the most perfect sacrifice and prayer.

To raise our hands is to express in a powerful way our part in the sacrifice of Christ, dependence on God, confidence in God, and openness to God. Psalm 77 says that my hands were raised at night without ceasing. In other words, I prayed all night long.

Strike Chest:

It was thought that the root of sin was in the heart, and to strike the chest was a sign of sorrow for sin. This gesture was common among ancient people and is found in the New Testament parable of the publican in Luke 18:13. It was also used as an expression of guilt by the witnesses of Jesus' crucifixion in Luke 23:48.

Clap Hands:

We find this in the Bible also. In Ezekiel 6:11 the Lord God says to clap your hands. And Psalm 47:2 says for all peoples to clap their hands.

Joined Hands:

129

We often pray with our hands joined; that is, palms together, thumbs crossed, fingers straight together and in front of our chest. This custom comes from the Middle Ages. Farmers needed protection from invaders who would steal their crops and rob their homes. These farmers looked for protection from powerful lords. These lords would protect them if they would give the lords a large portion of their crops, work the lord's lands or help to build and maintain their castles. The farmer would kneel in front of the lord with his hands joined. The lord would place his hands over the farmer's joined hands, and then the farmer would pledge loyalty and obedience to the lord. This gesture was a sign of submission because a person is helpless when the hands are together and surrounded by another person's hands. This arrangement was known as feudalism.

On the day of ordination to the priesthood, a man, with hands joined, kneels in front of the bishop who places his hands around the candidate's hands and asks, "Do you promise to be obedient to me and my successors?"

The gesture of joined hands is a symbol of our pledge of obedience to God and a symbol of our saying "yes" to whatever God wants or submitting to God's Will.

Stand:

In our culture, when a person of great dignity comes into the room, everyone stands out of respect. We also stand during times of prayer. The oldest position of the body for prayer was standing. Most religions used this position for hundreds of years, including Christianity. Many of the older churches do not have kneelers or pews. Some modern churches do not have kneelers. The Jews considered standing as the most fitting attitude for prayer and for listening to God's Word. The early Christians adopted this custom. It was a natural expression of respect, reverence and readiness. Standing straight, tall and free as baptized children of God had a special meaning for Christians. They had a new dignity. They were free from the slavery of sin and would rise from the dead.

Catholics stand at different times during the Liturgy to show respect.

Kneel:

For Catholics, kneeling is now the most popular position of the body in prayer. It has developed to be that way over the last few hundred years. However, the practice goes back to the Old Testament and is also found in many religions. In 1 Kings 8:54, when Solomon dedicated the Temple in Jerusalem, he prayed as he knelt. Kneeling is body language just as shaking hands is body language. In centuries past, men would shake hands so that both would know that the other had no weapon in their hand. Kneeling makes one helpless in the event of sudden trouble, and it shows a willingness to submit to the will of another. In the early Church, kneeling signified penance. In our relationship with God, kneeling expresses, in an admirable way, what our relationship with God should be; that is, we are helpless, and we are willing to bow down to His Will and do whatever He wants. Kneeling was practiced in the New Testament.

Here are a few scriptural references:

> After withdrawing about a stone's throw from them and kneeling, Jesus prayed. (Luke 22:41)

> Peter sent them all out and knelt down and prayed. (Acts 9:40)
> When he had finished speaking, Paul knelt down and prayed with them all. (Acts 20:36)
> All of the women and children included, escorted us out of the city, and after kneeling on the beach to pray, we bade farewell to one another. (Acts 21:6)
> Then Stephen knelt down … (Acts 7:60)

The early Christians, in the time of Tertullian, knelt for prayer except on Sundays and the Easter Season. As time went on, for Catholics, kneeling became more and more a sign of profound adoration, and that is its meaning today. The fact that Jesus Christ is present in the Blessed Sacrament is emphasized by the Catholic Church, and people come to adore Him. They kneel in adoration. The Liturgy of the Hours, prayed every day by priests, religious, and some lay people, begins with Psalm 95 which says to come and let us bow and bend low, and let us kneel before the God who made us.

Sit:

Sitting was the normal position of the official teacher, of a person who presided, of a judge or a person of special dignity in the presence of others of lower rank. A current example is when the Pope, as teacher, sits down while he delivers his talks. The Jews and early Christians used this position to listen to the readings and the sermons and to meditate. Standing was the usual position for prayer. Nowadays sitting is becoming a more common position for prayer. This has come about because of the introduction of pews into churches after the Protestant Movement of the 16th century.

Genuflection:

130

The word genuflection comes from two Latin words Genu, which is knee and flectere, which is to bend. So, to genuflect means to bend the knee. The gesture of bending the knee before someone dates back to pre-Christian times. It was an honor given to gods or rulers and especially to the Emperor. It was not used by the early Christians because of its pagan meaning. As time went on, this meaning was lost, and it began to be used as a sign of respect for those in high authority, like popes and bishops. For early Christians, the profound bow, rather than genuflection, was the usual act of adoration. This custom continues in the East.

In the 11th century, genuflection began to be used as an act of adoration of the Blessed Sacrament in reaction to the false teachings of Berengarius of Tours who did not believe that Jesus Christ is present in the Blessed Sacrament. Genuflection gradually became more popular, and Pope Pius V introduced it into the Mass in 1570.

Catholics genuflect, or bend the knee, before entering a pew. It is a sign of adoration and greeting towards Jesus Christ who is present in the Blessed Sacrament in the Tabernacle. Genuflection is a sign of reverence and respect. It was a gesture done in the kingly courts where one would make a profound bow, curtsy or genuflection when coming into the presence of royalty. Jesus, the King of Kings, is present in the Eucharist in the Tabernacle. We are supposed to genuflect whenever we pass in front of the Blessed Sacrament, whether in the Tabernacle or exposed on the altar for Adoration. To genuflect is a beautiful sign of our belief in the Real Presence of Jesus Christ in the Eucharist. St. Paul says in his letter to Philippians 2:10, that at the name of Jesus every knee must bend. The Eucharist is Jesus Christ Himself, and so it is even more appropriate to bend the knee, or genuflect, in front of Him.

Some people say that we should replace genuflection with a bow. This is not the tradition in the Church in the West. To bow is customary in the church in the East. In our age and culture, genuflection makes a particularly strong statement. After all, people bow to one another all the time, but we bend the knee only to God.

SACRED VESSELS

Sacred Vessels:

There are several containers or vessels used in liturgical worship. Most of them originated from practical utensils that, because of their use in the Liturgy, came to be regarded as sacred. They were set apart from common use by blessings or consecrations and were often decorated.

131

Chalice:

At Mass the Priest uses something like a goblet. This is a chalice. It is the most necessary of all the liturgical vessels. In it the wine is consecrated or changed into the Blood of Christ at Mass. It is the only vessel mentioned in all four scriptural accounts of the institution of the Eucharist by Jesus Christ. Early chalices were like the drinking vessels normally used and were distinguished from these only by ornamentation. They were made from any metal, and chalices of glass, wood, or horn were not unknown. Since the 9th century, however, only precious metals have been used.

Paten:

The Priest also uses a golden plate. The plate is called a paten. The paten is a shallow plate on which the large host rests. Originally it was a very large dish made of metal or wood, and from it the Eucharist was given to the people. By the ninth century fewer people were receiving Holy Communion, so the paten was reduced in size, and in time took on its present form, a small plate.

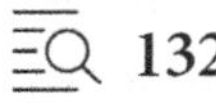 132

Monstrance:

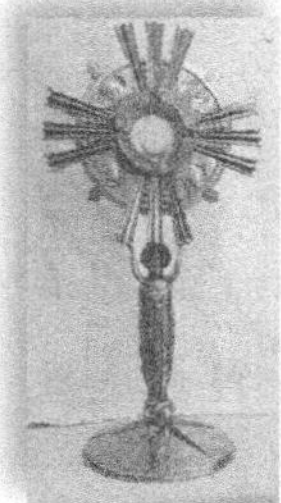

During Adoration, the Host is put in a tall decorated vessel. This is a monstrance. The name comes from the Latin word monstrare which is to show. The monstrance is a sacred vessel used for showing of the Blessed Sacrament at Exposition, Benediction, and in processions. It was first used in France and Germany during the 13th and 14th centuries as a result of devotion to the Real Presence of Jesus Christ in the Blessed Sacrament and also as a result of the institution of the Feast of Corpus Christi or The Body of Christ (see Exposition).

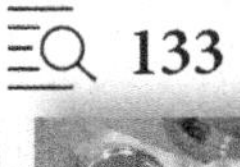 133

Pyx:

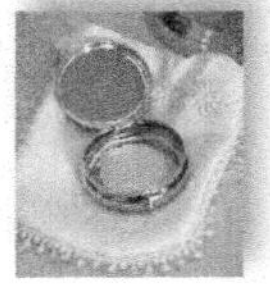

Holy Communion is brought to the sick in a small box which is called a pyx. It is a container for the Blessed Sacrament. It was at first a small wooden box, usually round and with a lid.

During the Middle Ages, the pyx was sometimes made of metal or ivory. When containing the Blessed Sacrament, it was left at first in peoples' houses, later it was left in the sacristy, then on the altar. Later still, it was suspended above the altar, sometimes inside a metal dove. A locked box in the wall was later introduced. This was called an ambry which comes from a Latin word meaning a safe or arms-chest. When sacrament houses and tabernacles came into use for keeping the Blessed Sacrament, the pyx underwent two changes.

The first change was to make it bigger, and place it on a stand, making it what we now call a ciborium, from the Latin word cibus which is food. We receive food from the ciborium when we receive the Body of Christ. A ciborium is a vessel like a chalice. It contains the hosts which have been changed into the Body of Christ at Mass. The second change was to make the pyx smaller and add a lid with a hinge. The pyx can hold only a few hosts for the sick.

Tabernacle: 134

There is a golden box in Catholic Churches. It is called a tabernacle. A tabernacle is a decorated container, which used to be attached to the altar. It contains the Sacred Hosts reserved for Communion for the sick and for the laity outside of Mass and for Adoration.

The Blessed Sacrament has been preserved or kept in different ways and places over the centuries. Sometimes the Host was reserved in the churches or elsewhere. In churches, the Host was placed in the sacristy, in a recess in the wall or in a sacrament house. In other places, the Host was placed in a movable vessel like a tower, pyx, or metal dove. The pyx or the metal dove would be placed near the altar or hanging above the altar.

Only in 1614 did the tabernacle, placed on the main altar, begin to be the normal manner of reservation of the Blessed Sacrament. In 1863, all other ways of reservation were forbidden. In recent years, the Blessed Sacrament is kept in a special chapel or in a place of honor in a church.

The word tabernacle comes from the Latin word tabernaculum which is a tent or a small hut. In the Old Testament, the tabernacle was a tent which the Israelites carried around with them as they wandered in the desert after leaving Egypt. God would come in the form of a cloud to this Tent of Meeting to talk with Moses. In the early days of Christianity there were no tabernacles like we have in parishes today. Nowadays we go to the tabernacle to talk with Jesus Christ, who is present in the tabernacle under the appearance of bread, just as Moses went to the tabernacle, or Tent of Meeting, to talk with God

VESTMENTS

Vestments:

In the Old Testament Book of Exodus 28:2-5, God speaks to Moses. He says that you will make sacred vestments for your brother Aaron to give him dignity and magnificence. You will instruct all the skilled men, whom I have endowed with skill, to make Aaron's vestments for his consecration to My priesthood. And God said these are the vestments, which they must make: a pectoral, an ephod, a robe, an embroidered tunic, a turban and a belt. They must make sacred vestments for your brother, Aaron, and his sons for them to be priests in My service. They will use gold and violet material, red, purple and crimson, and finely woven linens.

The remainder of this section gives details about each vestment. There is nothing in the New Testament which requires the discontinuation of ministerial vestments. Jesus did condemn the Jewish leaders for their sins, but never condemned their priestly vestments. The early Church did not use the Old Testament vestments because the Christians did not want to identify their leaders with the Jewish priesthood. Some maintain that priests adopted different clothing in the 4th century in order to put themselves above the laity. However, in fact, it was the laity who changed their clothing in order to keep up with the fashions of the day. The vestments the priests wear today have their origin in fashions of the Greco-Roman world, and they have taken on liturgical meaning over the centuries.

Colors:

135

GREEN;
WHITE or
GOLD or
SILVER;
RED;
PURPLE
BLACK

Various colored vestments are worn at Mass. Green is worn in Ordinary Time, the times between special church seasons. It symbolizes hope, everlasting life and fidelity. White is worn at Easter, Christmas, and feasts of Our Lord, Our Lady and saints who are not martyrs. It symbolizes joy. Gold or silver can be worn instead of white. Red is worn at Pentecost and other feasts of the Holy Spirit, Good Friday, and feasts of martyrs. It symbolizes suffering. Purple is worn in Advent and Lent. It signifies penance, repentance, and mourning. Black can be worn for funerals.

Alb:

136–137

It is a long white garment worn by clerics. It gets its name from the Latin word albus which is white. The alb can be traced directly to the early Roman citizens who wore it as an everyday garment. The alb was covered by a cloak or tunic. It was first mentioned in early Christian writings about 260-270 A.D. Pope St. Sylvester (d. 335) instituted the long sleeved alb, the type that is used today. The alb's design was not changed from the 4th century until the latter part of the 20th century when modern convenience and design allowed for the use of zippers, snaps, buttons, and velcro.

The alb must be white. In 1207, Pope Innocent III decreed that the alb would represent the purity of the clerical state and be a symbol of the cleric's baptismal state. The cleric, as he puts on the alb, prays, "Cleanse me, Lord, and purify my heart, so that being washed in the Blood of the Lamb, I may come to enjoy everlasting bliss."

Cincture:

The cincture is a cord worn around the waist and is used to keep the alb close to the body. It is generally white. It is a symbol of self-restraint or abstinence. As he puts on the cincture the cleric prays, "Gird me, Lord, with the cincture of purity and extinguish within me unholy desires, so that I may persevere in continence and chastity."

Stole:

138

The word stole comes from a Greek word meaning towel. Originally the stole was used as a scarf to keep the neck and upper body warm. It was also used to cover the face of a dead person before the body was wrapped in the burial shroud. By the 4th century, in Roman society, the stole was used as a sign of dignity, much like public honors. A person who performed special services for the state was entitled to wear a stole. If one performed heroic deeds for the state, they could wear a colored stole over the alb.

By the 6th century, it was worn by bishops. In 813 A.D., the Council of Mayence decreed that all clerics were required to wear a stole. Bishops and priests wear the stole, like a scarf, around the back of the neck with each side of the stole falling equally in front. Deacons wear it over the left shoulder, across the chest, to the right hip. The stole is like a yoke which reminds the cleric of his promise or vow of obedience, and that he is attached to Jesus Christ. The priest wears a stole when he is representing Christ in the administration of the Sacraments. It is a symbol of his authority, as it was for the Romans. The cleric, as he puts on the stole, prays, "Restore to me, Lord, the stole of immortality which was lost through the transgression of our first parents; and unfit though I be to approach your Sacred Mystery, let me be worthy at last of eternal joy."

Maniple:

139

The maniple was a cloth, made of linen which was carried on the wrist and was used in Rome to wipe away perspiration from one's brow, hands and lips. Over time it became what we call today a napkin. It also came to be the purificator which is used to clean the chalice and ciborium at Mass. As time went on, it was made of the same material and color as the chasuble. By the 14th century, it was purely a symbol and was set aside by the reforms of Pope Paul VI. It continues to be used today in the extraordinary rite, or the Tridentine Mass. The cleric, as he puts on the maniple, prays, "May I have the grace, Lord, to bear the maniple of tears and sorrow, so that I may receive with delight the reward of my labor."

Chasuble:

The Latin word for chasuble, or cloak, is casula meaning a little house. In the Greek and Roman culture, a cloak was worn over the alb when a man left his home. This vestment is a symbol of being sheltered or protected from evil. In the early Church, the priests used everyday clothing while offering the Mass, and only gradually began to use more costly clothing for that purpose.

The chasuble is the outer vestment worn by the priest at Mass and is derived from the cloak, or casula, of the worker or farmer. It was like a modern-day poncho, which protected the wearer from the weather. It had a seam in the front, so that the farmer could see what he was doing as he worked his fields, even when it was raining. It also had a hood. This type of garment was worn by the peasant classes as far back as 300 B.C.

By the 3rd century A.D., the casula was worn by all Christians. Soon, the casula was considered to be a sacred vestment and reserved for bishops and priests. When the barbarians, who wore pants, invaded the Roman Empire, they brought about a change in the clothing styles. However, the priests continued to wear the garments they had always worn for Mass.

The earliest chasuble had a hood, but this was abolished for sacred vestments. In 633 A.D., the Council of Toledo decreed that the chasuble was to be the official vestment for all bishops and priests, and the dalmatic, a coat or cloak with sleeves, was to be the official vestment for deacons. The chasuble started off as a simple cloak, but as the years went on different kinds of embroidery were added to make it more magnificent for the offering of the Sacrifice of the Mass.

So, the vestments worn by the priests celebrating Mass today are the kind that were worn in the early Church Masses. The priest, as he puts on the chasuble, prays, "O Lord, who said, 'My yoke is easy and my burden light,' help me to carry it in such a way as to win your favor. Amen."

Cope: 141

The cope is a long mantle or cloak. This is a vestment worn by clergy at different rites, such as Benediction, solemn Liturgy of the Hours and Processions. It is worn around the shoulders, extends to the floor, open in the front and is fastened at the chest by a clasp. A hood, shaped like a shield, is usually on the back of the cope. Beautiful embroidery often decorates the vestment. The cope originates from the Roman raincoat.

Humeral Veil: 142

The humeral veil is a cloth, eight or nine feet long and two to three feet wide, draped over the shoulders and down the front. It is fastened with clasps or ribbons. It has been used for some liturgical ceremonies at least since the 8th century. The humeral veil is usually used with the cope and is the same color, material and style as the cope. The humeral veil is worn to show reverence for the sacred object which is being carried in Procession, such as the Blessed Sacrament or relics, or when the people are being blessed with them.

The minister covers his hands with the ends of the veil so that his hands do not touch the monstrance containing the Blessed Sacrament. This indicates that it is Christ, not the priest or deacon, who blesses.

FASTING

Fasting: 143

Most religions have days of fasting. Catholics fast also. Fasting was practiced in the Church from Apostolic times. It was much more severe than it is today. Up to the 10th century, during Lent and other special occasions, some of the faithful kept an absolute fast until sunset, and then their meal consisted of bread and vegetables. Water was not used during the day in some places. Mass would be celebrated in the evening, and only after this, was food allowed.

Today, there are only two days of fasting in the year, Ash Wednesday and Good Friday. A person is allowed one full meal and two smaller meals, and no meat on those two days.

No Meat on Fridays:

144

Catholics did not eat meat on Fridays. Abstinence signifies depriving ourselves of meat, so that the body may practice penance and the soul be made more holy. The Church had days of abstinence from the time of the Apostles. Friday was one of those days because Jesus died on that day for our sins.

Up until recently, abstinence from meat on Fridays was considered a very serious obligation, and it was even one of the distinguishing ways people would recognize Catholics. Pope Paul VI reduced the severity of abstinence in 1966, but some form of penance is encouraged on Fridays. The rule of abstinence is still in force during the Fridays of Lent.

Fast and Abstinence:

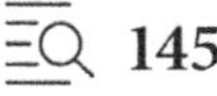 145

Christians, from the beginning, practiced fasting (limiting the amount of food) and abstaining (avoiding certain kinds of foods). Abstaining from meat is a tradition in Christian spirituality. The Jews had the tradition long before Christianity began. For example, Daniel and his friends rejected meat, which was offered to them by the king. They chose vegetables instead (Daniel 1:8-16).

The idea behind abstaining from meat was not to imply that meat was bad, but it was to do penance, to share in the sufferings of Christ and to discipline our bodies. Throughout history meat has been more expensive and more desirable. Trying to obtain meat can open us up more easily to temptations.

Fish:

146

Some people enjoy fish more than meat. The church tries to deal with what generally happens in daily life. Since meat is commonly more delightful and luxurious than fish, even though some people would not agree, the church focuses its attention more on meat. We must always remember that the prayers, fasting and almsgiving that we especially practice during Lent are not ends in themselves and not done to make us feel good. We observe fast and abstinence, especially during Lent, in order to imitate Jesus Christ and to prepare ourselves for a more joyous celebration of the mysteries of our redemption during Easter.

Fasting, or the limiting of the amount of food we eat, has many advantages: First, Jesus fasted and expects His followers to fast; Second, fasting slows us down. We realize that we depend on food, which gives us energy; Third, we are more in solidarity with the poor who have little or nothing to eat; Fourth, through fasting God comes into our lives in a stronger way, and we become more humble; Fifth, we become more conscious of the wonderful gifts God has lavished upon us.

PART FIVE

PRACTICES, CUSTOMS, TRADITIONS, WORSHIP, ETC.

Having explained some of the symbols in the Catholic Church we now endeavor to explain some of the customs, practices, traditions, worship, places, times, etc. of the Church.

CODE OF CANON LAW

Code of Canon Law

The Code of Canon Law is a book of the laws of the Catholic Church which are based on Scripture, Synods (gatherings of clergy), writings of the Church Fathers, papal decrees, Roman laws, etc. In 1140 a monk, Gratian, gathered all this information into one huge volume. One hundred years later, St. Raymond of Penyafort (1175-1275) compiled another volume of relevant information. These two volumes were combined. The need to revise and simplify these works was realized by the Council of Trent (1545-1563).

This became the Code of Canon Law and was published in 1917. St. John XXIII and Pope Paul VI realized that the 1917 Code should be updated, and this gave rise to the 1983 Code which was published by St. John Paul II.

CATECHISM

Catechism:

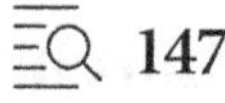
147

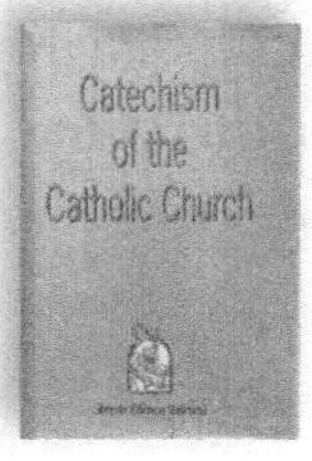

The first Catechism was written in question and answer form by Martin Luther in 1529. Pope Pius V completed the Roman Catechism in 1566 under the authority of the Council of Trent. It was not a question and answer catechism, but a collection of essays directed to parish priests and divided into four sections: (1) The Creed; (2) The Sacraments; (3) The Commandments; (4) The Our Father. The new *Catechism of the Catholic Church*, promulgated by St. John Paul II, was published in 1992 and follows the same headings. Each paragraph is numbered in the *Catechism of the Catholic Church*. When you see CCC 692, this refers you to paragraph 692 which explains The Titles of the Holy Spirit.

The first Catholic Catechism was written by St. Peter Canisius for Germany in 1566. In Italy, St. Robert Bellarmine wrote a small Catechism for children in 1597 and one for teachers in 1598. In 1884 the Council of Baltimore set into motion the Baltimore Catechism. It was written by Fr. Vincent De Consilio, of Jersey City, New Jersey and Bishop John Lancaster Spalding of Peoria, Ill. They relied on a catechism by George Hay of Edinburgh (1778) and an Irish Catechism published in 1775 by Archbishop James Butler, which was revised by the Synod of Maynooth in 1885. The Baltimore Catechism had 421 questions and answers, which dealt with Catholic doctrine and practice. Millions of Catholic children learned about the Catholic faith from this Catechism during the following 80 years.

Emblem of the Catechism of the Catholic Church 147

Most versions of the *Catechism of the Catholic Church* have this Emblem on the cover or inside cover page.

This image of the Good Shepherd is to be found in the Catacombs of Domitilla in Rome. It depicts Jesus as the Good Shepherd who lays down His Life for His sheep.

CHURCHES

Churches First Built: 148

The persecution of the Catholic Christians ended in 313 A.D., and churches were built after that. One of the oldest Catholic Churches is still in Antioch.

Facing East:

149

In the early centuries of Catholicism, the Churches were built facing towards the East. Mass was celebrated with the priest and people also facing East. Mt. 24:27 explains, as lightening comes from the East … so shall the Son of Man appear. This is the scriptural basis for the Christian belief that when Jesus Christ comes again in glory, He will come from the East. This is why there is an ancient Christian practice of facing East while praying.

In the 4th century, St. Basil wrote that it was one of the most ancient traditions of the Church at the time. The East represents Christ, so when we pray facing East, we pray facing Christ. The East also represents heaven because it is the place from which Christ will return. So, facing the East implies a longing for Christ's second coming.

The same idea is in the Old Testament. In Ezekiel 43:1-4, the angel led the prophet to the gate which faces East, and there he saw the glory of the God of Israel coming and entering the temple by the gate facing East.

Steeple:

150

Steeples were attached to a church during the Middle Ages so that the church could be seen from any part of the town. At that time the Church was the heart of the town. The steeple was built to be the tallest structure in town to remind everyone of the Church's importance in their lives. People would not build a structure higher than the Church as a sign of respect for God.

Pews:

151

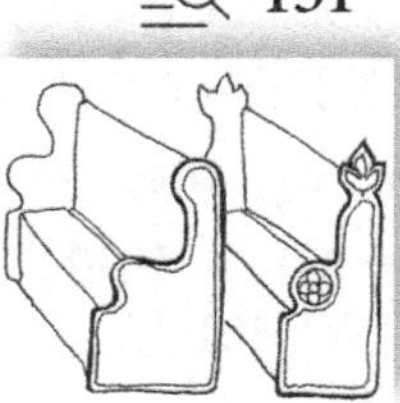

Originally there was a chair for the presider, who was a bishop or priest, and there was no other furniture in the churches. As time went on, stone seats began to be attached to the walls or to the pillars. By the end of the 13th century, many churches in England had some wooden benches, often called pews.

Pews were introduced into churches in the 16th century by Protestant churches. During their services, the emphasis was on listening to Scripture and preaching. To sit indicates listening and resting. Pews became more common as printing became more common. We went from a manuscript culture (where books were rare and more often heard than read) to a print culture (with wide distribution of books).

The Orthodox custom is to stand, which indicates praising God with upright bodies. It is not known when kneelers began to be attached to the pews. The Catholic custom is to kneel, which indicates adoration or penitence. The Protestant custom is to sit, which indicates listening respectfully and participating in a common meal.

Chair:

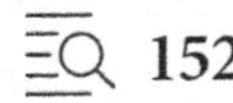

Judges and teachers traditionally exercised their office while seated. Consequently, the chair became a symbol of authority. Jewish religious leaders said that they had the authority to interpret Jewish practices and beliefs in an unbroken line going back to Moses. The Chair of Moses is an symbol of this teaching authority. Some synagogues had a chair symbolizing this belief.

The Chair of Peter is a theological expression for the teaching authority of the Pope. Cathedra is the Latin word for chair, and when the Pope exercises his full teaching authority, he is said to speak ex cathedra or from the chair. The word cathedral comes from the same Latin word. The cathedral is the bishop's church, and the bishop is the chief teacher in his diocese.

Pulpit:

Probably the oldest reference we have about a pulpit in the Old Testament is in Nehemiah where it says that Ezra, the scribe, stood on a wooden platform, built for the occasion, when he read from the book of the Law to the people (Neh 8:1-12). That happened about 442 B.C.

Relics:

A relic is part of the physical remains of a saint; for example, a piece of bone, or an object closely associated with a saint, such as clothing or something used by a saint. Even in early Christian times, the Christians venerated authentic relics of saints. The Church still holds to that belief.

Relics of martyrs were placed in stones inserted into fixed altars. The Church, however, condemns superstition and simony, which is the making of money from spiritual things. Why do Catholics use relics? Relics somehow put us spiritually in touch with Our Lord or the saints. They help us to meditate on the holiness or heroism of the saints, and they help us to love God and His friends, the saints, more fervently. The same idea is behind the collecting of a football shirt worn by a famous player or an autographed football. Catholics treasure relics in much the same way.

Relics are divided into three types: First Class Relics which consist of the bodily remains of the saints or the instruments of the passion of Christ, such as the True Cross; Second Class Relics which are the personal belongings of saints, such as articles of clothing, things they used, etc.; Third Class Relics which are objects that have been touched to a First or Second Class Relic. We must remember that Catholics are not compelled to venerate any particular relics, but that veneration of relics is proper. The Council of Trent said that the honor given in reference to a relic, statue, or icon was honor given NOT to that object itself (which would be idolatry) but honor given to the person represented by the object.

The Bible gives an account of the use of relics. In the Old Testament in 2 Kings 2:13-14, we find that the prophet Elisha had just witnessed his teacher, Elijah, taken up into heaven. He saw that Elijah's cloak had fallen on the ground. He picked it up and put it on. He went to the Jordan River, called upon the God of Elijah, struck the water with the cloak, and the river parted for him to cross over. This is an example of the power of God coming through the relic of a saint who had departed from this world.

God also used the physical remains of saints to give His grace to others. In 2 Kings 13:20-21, we read that after the prophet Elisha died, some Israelites were burying a man. When they saw a band of raiders coming, they threw the man's body into Elisha's tomb. When the body touched Elisha's bones, the man came to life and stood up.

The ancient Jews treated the remains of their ancestors with the greatest of respect. In Gen 50:25, Joseph made his family swear that they would take his body with them when they would leave Egypt to return to the Promised Land. Four hundred years later, Moses did bring Joseph's body to the Promised Land in Exodus 13:19. In Exodus 16:33, Moses instructs Aaron to place a jar of manna inside the Ark of the Covenant. In Exodus 25:21, the Ten Commandments are also put into the Ark. Hebrews 9:4 said the rod of Aaron was put into the Ark. So, the Ark, the holiest object in Israel, was a place where relics were kept.

God works miracles through objects. God can do whatever He wants to do. Let us take examples from the New Testament: in Lk 6:18-19, those troubled by evil spirits were cured, and the people all tried to touch Jesus because power was coming from Him and healing them all; in Lk 8:40-48, the woman who touched the tassel of Jesus' garment is healed of the hemorrhage she had endured for twelve years.

But, was the woman guilty of superstition? Certainly not. Jesus' clothing did not work magic. On account of the faith of the woman, Jesus used the garment as the vehicle of healing for the woman. Jesus said, "I know power has gone out from Me." It was Jesus' power, and not magic in the garment that healed the woman.

In Matthew 14:35-36, we are told that the people of Gennesaret brought their sick to Jesus and begged Him to let the sick just touch the edge of His cloak. All who touched it were healed. Jesus used His garment as a vehicle for His healing power.

Altar:

155

God is honored in many ways. A special way of honoring Him is by offering sacrifice on an altar to Him. Genesis 22: 9-10 is the story of Abraham building an altar and being willing to sacrifice his son, Isaac, on it. Abraham went to Canaan 3,000 years ago. Archeologists have found Canaanite altars which existed 1,000 years before Abraham. So, before the time of Abraham, it was common throughout the Middle East to worship by burning sacrifice.

Let us look. In the Old Covenant with Abraham, animals and grain could be burned on the altar. At times the whole gift was offered to God in the fire, and at other times only parts of the animal were burned. The remainder was given to the priests, or to the person making the offering who consumed it in a sacred meal. This meal set up a union between God and the person eating it.

In Old Testament times there were many different kinds of altars. Some were made of earth which were built up, and others were made of stones. Some were small, probably for burning incense. Some were large. Animal sacrifices were offered in the open air on account of the smoke and odor of burning animals. It was only at the Temple in Jerusalem that animal sacrifices were offered. All this ended with the destruction of the Temple by the Romans in 70 A.D.

Jesus celebrated the Passover meal and changed it into something new. He changed bread and wine into His Body, Blood, Soul and Divinity. He told His Apostles, "Do this in memory of me." The early Christians went to the Temple every day, and then to their homes for the breaking of the bread (Acts 2:46-47).

The Christians decided that they did not need the kind of altar used in the Temple since they were not offering that kind of sacrifice. They were doing what Jesus commanded them to do at the Last Supper, and so they used a table in their homes. In the 2nd Century the celebration of the Eucharist was separated from the common meal, probably on account of the Eucharist being a sacrifice. They began to realize that it was not simply a meal, or a sacrifice, but a sacrificial meal.

In the 4th century the Emperor, Constantine, was converted to Christianity, so the Christians were no longer persecuted, and churches could be built. Some of these churches had wooden altars. The wooden tables in the homes were being replaced by wooden and stone altars in churches. The stone altars were very much like the stone slab over the graves of the martyrs on which the Eucharist was offered, and also, they were a reminder of the stone altars of the Old Covenant with Abraham.

The leaders of the Protestant Movement emphasized the meal aspect of their services, while the Catholic Church defended the sacrificial aspect of the Mass. This is reflected in the architecture of the Catholic churches where the altars are more like altars of sacrifice than tables.

Since the 2nd Vatican Council (1962-65), the emphasis is on the Eucharist as a sacrificial banquet, and the new altars attempt to reflect this. The Church reminds us that the altar is a sign of Christ. To show the utmost respect, the altar is anointed, incensed and kissed. Here God comes to man and man to God as the covenant is daily renewed in meal and sacrifice. The table aspect of the altar reminds us of the Last Supper, the family meal with Christ, our Brother. The stone aspect of the altar resembles Christ's Sacrifice, which continues today. The altar is a symbol of Christ's meal and sacrifice, which is the source and summit of the Christian Life.

Chapel:

A chapel is a place of prayer for the convenience of an individual or small group of people; for example, a bishop's private chapel, or the chapel in a seminary or convent. It can be used as a public oratory in a hospital, university, or airport. It is a building, or part of a building, set aside for prayer services, especially the Mass. Some large churches may have small chapels dedicated for specific purposes; for example, for Adoration of the Blessed Sacrament or in honor of Our Lady.

The word chapel comes from the Latin word cappa, meaning small cape or cloak. Its origin goes back to the year 334 A.D. A young Roman soldier named Martin (317-397) saw a beggar shivering in the cold. He took his own cloak, cut it in half, gave one half to the beggar, and put the other half over his own shoulders as a small cape. That night Martin had a dream in which he saw Christ wearing the half of the cloak he had given to the beggar. He realized that the beggar was Christ in disguise. Martin converted to Catholicism, became a monk, an abbot, and finally the bishop of Tours in France. Today, he is known as St. Martin of Tours.

After Martin's death, his small cape was kept in a tent called the capella, and the priests who offered Mass in that tent each day were called capellani. From these old French words, we get the words chapel and chaplain.

Icons:

156

Eikon is the Greek work for image or icon. An icon is a painting of Our Lord, Our Lady, or a saint on a wooden panel or a wall. It is used in devotions. The process of painting an icon is called icon writing. It is called writing because the artist first has his hands blessed and then asks the Lord to take his hands and use them to write what He, the Lord, wants on the painting to teach or to tell a story to those who could not read or could not acquire books. Each symbol on the icons has a meaning. For example, three stars are on some icons of the Mother of Jesus symbolizing the fact that Mary retained her virginity before, during and after the birth of Jesus Christ. One picture can say a thousand words.

The Eastern Churches utilize icons. The Catholic Church utilizes icons and statues. Images, icons or statues, when used properly, become physical pointers to Christ, who is the image of God Whom we cannot see.

Councils of the Church:

A council is a formal meeting of church leaders, called together by the proper church authority to study and clarify the beliefs or practices of the Church. They were called to clarify a teaching or to deal with doctrinal or pastoral issues.

The first council of the Church was held in Jerusalem in 51 A.D. The person in charge of that council was St. Peter (Acts 15:6). It was decided that Gentiles, or non-Jews, who converted to Christianity, did not have to abide by Jewish customs (Acts 15:22-29).

There have been many councils in the Church, but only 21 were called Ecumenical or Universal starting with the Council of Nicaea in 325 and ending with Vatican II in 1962-65. A council is never ecumenical unless it is confirmed, or at least accepted, as such, by the Pope. There were 2500 bishops from all over the world at the Second Vatican Council. The Orthodox Churches recognize only the first seven councils from First Council of Nicaea in 325 to Second Council of Nicaea in 787.

The Holy See:

157

These words describe Rome or the place where the Pope is bishop. The word see comes from the Latin word sedes, which is seat, or the place where a bishop dwells. The bishop's office is symbolized by the chair in which he presides over his people. The word see is applied to all dioceses.

Statues:

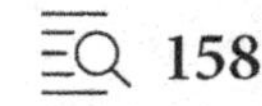

158

There are statues in Catholic churches. But, in the Book of Exodus 20:4-6, God said not to make a graven (carved or sculptured) image or any likeness of anything that is in heaven above, or that is in the earth beneath, or that is in the water under the earth. And He said not to bow down to them or serve them. Five chapters after this, God gave Moses strict instructions as to how to build the Ark of the Covenant. In Exodus 25:17-19, God commands Moses to make graven images. Also, in 1 Kings 6:12-35, God commands Solomon to make images of things in both heaven above and the earth beneath when he built the house for the Lord. The cedar was carved in the form of gourds and flowers. Two cherubim of olivewood were in the inner sanctuary. The walls were carved with figures of cherubim, palm trees and flowers. The Ark of the Covenant would be placed in the inner part of the Temple, which Solomon was building. God commanded Solomon to place the graven (carved) cherubim on the Ark.

In Numbers 21:8-9, God commanded Moses to make a fiery serpent and set it on a pole so that those who were bitten by serpents could look at it and be healed.

God did want the Israelites and us to have statues and images. What He definitely did not want was for us to worship or serve these statues. This has always been the teaching of the Catholic Church. The statues simply remind us of God, Mary, the angels and saints just as the Statue of Liberty reminds us of the United States and its values.

Catholics have statues in churches, in their homes, outdoors and so on. Do Catholics believe that statues have special powers? Certainly not. No statues have any power in and of themselves. These statues just serve to lead us to God. God created man as a being who is both spiritual AND physical. God gave us BOTH spiritual and physical means to draw us to Himself, and statues are a physical means. There was disagreement in the Church from the beginning as to whether statues and icons were acceptable. Their use grew among the people.

Between 726 and 843, there was turmoil in the Church in the East. Some people broke statues and icons in churches. During the Protestant Revolt in the 16th century the matter was settled. Lutherans and Orthodox agreed that Nicaea II (787) confirmed the teachings of the earlier councils that images were not being adored as divine but honored as sacred objects. Statues and icons could be used.

Today, Protestants object to statues, and Catholics use them as reminders of Jesus Christ, Mary, angels and saints. Catholics do not worship statues just as Americans do not worship the Statue of Liberty, or the statues which have been erected throughout the country in honor of great heroes.

TIMES TO HONOR GOD

All cultures honored their gods each day, each month, and each year. Catholics honor God in these ways also. In the Book of Genesis, God put forward the idea of time being divided into 7-day periods. God created everything in 6 days, and then rested on the 7th day.

Several thousand years ago, by studying the stars, the Egyptians made a calendar with a year of 365 days. There have been many changes since then. Our calendar today has been developed from the one the Egyptians had. A lunar month on the Egyptian calendar was calculated 29 or 30 days, and each month began with the full moon. This was divided into 4 periods, which we now call weeks. The Babylonians divided their calendar into four weeks. The first three weeks had seven days, and the last week had 8 or 9 days. The idea of a 7-day week was adopted by the Greeks, and they named the days after the sun, moon and five planets which they could see with the naked eye. The planets were named after their gods.

In pagan cultures, these lights in the heavens were honored as gods. The names of the days of the week were later adopted throughout the Greek and Roman world. The Germanic peoples invaded the Roman Empire bringing with them their own Nordic culture. They renamed four days of the week, Tuesday, Wednesday, Thursday and Friday, after their own Norse gods. Those names came down to us. Catholics dedicate each day of the week and each month of the year to some aspect of their faith.

Sunday:

159

Sunday, the first day of the week, is named after the sun. Day comes from the Old English word daeg. Pagans honored the sun god, but Christians honor the Son of God. It was on Sunday that Jesus Christ rose from the dead, and on Sunday that the Holy Spirit descended upon the Apostles at the first Pentecost. This day of the week is dedicated by Catholics to the Holy Trinity.

Monday:

160

Monday is named in honor of the moon, Moonday or the day of the Moon. Monday is dedicated by Catholics to the souls in Purgatory.

Tuesday:

161

Tuesday got its name from a Germanic Norse god, Tiw or Tyr, or Day of Tyr. Tyr was the Norse god of war, law and justice. Catholics dedicate this day to our Guardian Angel.

Wednesday: 162

Wednesday, or Wodensday, is also named after a god. Woden, called Odin, was the chief god of the Norse peoples. He was the war god and protector of heroes. Wednesday is the day on which Judas betrayed Jesus. From the early centuries of Christianity, Wednesday was a day of fasting, and is dedicated to St. Joseph.

Thursday: 163

Thursday, or Thor's Day, is named in honor of the Norse god Thor, the god of thunder. Catholics place emphasis on the fact that Jesus Christ instituted the Eucharist and ordained His first priests on Thursday. Thursday is dedicated to the Holy Eucharist.

Friday: 164

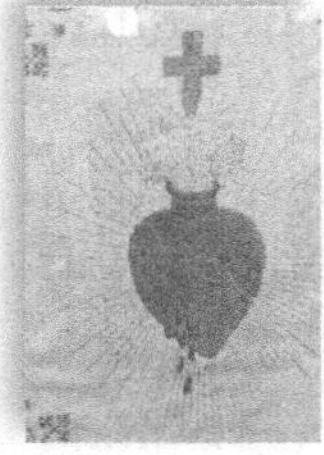

Friday, Freya's Day, is named in honor of the Norse goddess of love, Fria or Freya. Catholics honor this day as the day Jesus Christ died on the cross to open heaven for us. The Catholic Church encourages us to do some type of penance on this day. Friday is dedicated to the Precious Blood of Jesus Christ.

Saturday: 165

Saturday or the Day of Saturn, is named after the planet Saturn. Saturn is the Roman god of agriculture. Catholics set this day aside to honor the Blessed Virgin Mary.

January: 166

Catholics also dedicate each month of the year to some aspect of their faith. The month of January takes its name from Janus, a Roman god of beginnings or transitions. Janus has two faces looking in opposite directions, one to the past and one to the future. The word also denoted gates or doors. The Catholic Church concentrates on beginnings, and the beginning of the life of Jesus Christ. So, the month of January is dedicated to the Holy Childhood.

February:

167

The month of February comes from the Latin word Februarius. February is the cleansing and purifying month. The Roman feast of the expiation or atonement was celebrated on the 15th of the month, probably in preparation for the Roman new year which began in March. The Catholic Church dedicates February to the Holy Family.

March:

168

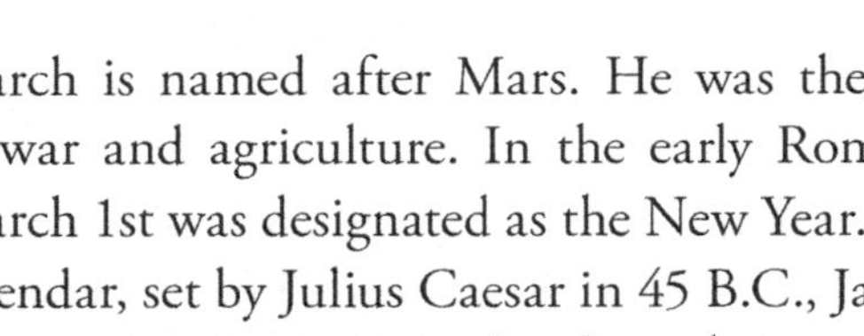

March is named after Mars. He was the Roman god of war and agriculture. In the early Roman calendar, March 1st was designated as the New Year. In the Julian calendar, set by Julius Caesar in 45 B.C., January 1st was the New Year. However, by the 15th century, the calendar was off by ten days. In 1582, Pope Gregory XIII reformed the calendar dropping the ten days from the calendar in October. He added a Leap Year every four years to maintain accuracy in the calendar, and he kept January 1st as the New Year. We now follow the calendar of Pope Gregory XIII. The Catholic Church dedicates March to St. Joseph, the husband of Mary and the foster father of Jesus. His solemn feast day is March 19th.

April:

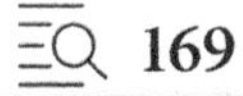

April is named in honor of a goddess also. April is named after Aperire which means to open. In the spring, the buds open. Some say that April may be named after Aphrodite, the Greek goddess of love. Catholics dedicate April to the Holy Spirit and the Holy Eucharist.

May: 170

May is the month of Our Lady. May comes from the Latin name Maius derived from the Greek goddess, Maia, mother of Mercury and daughter of Atlas.

The Romans also had a goddess named Maia. She was a vague but powerful Roman goddess of Spring and growth, and she was explicitly identified with the earth (Terra) goddess. She was paired with Vulcan, the Roman god of fire and metalwork, whose priests offered sacrifice to Maia on the first day of May. May Day reigns as one of the oldest holidays in Western European tradition. Catholics dedicate May to the Blessed Virgin Mary.

June: 171

June comes from the 4th month of the ancient calendar attributed to Romulus, the legendary founder and first king of Rome. June may also be named after Juno, an important Roman goddess. She was queen of the goddesses and the heavens. Juno is patroness of marriage and married couple's households. June also comes from the Latin word, Juvenis, young people. Catholics dedicate June to the Sacred Heart of Jesus.

July: 172

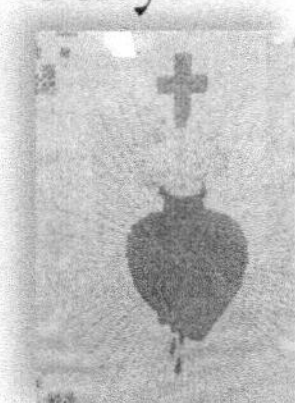

July is named from Julius Caesar, a Roman general and statesman born in July, 100 B.C. Catholics dedicate this month to the Precious Blood of Jesus.

August: 173

August is named after Caesar Augustus (63 B.C. to 14 A.D.), who was the first Roman Emperor and grandnephew of Julius Caesar. Augustus means venerable, noble, and majestic. Catholics dedicate August to the Blessed Sacrament.

September, October, November, December: 174-177

The last four months of our year are named after the seventh, eighth, ninth and tenth months of the ancient Roman calendar.

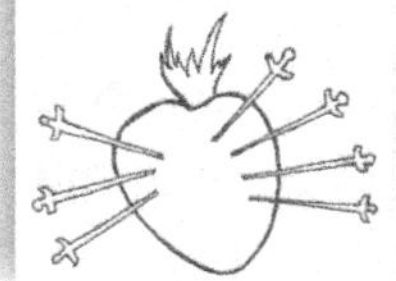

September is taken from the Latin word septem which is seven. The Romans looked upon March as the first month of the year, so, for them, September would be the seventh month.

Catholics have dedicated September to the Seven Sorrows of Our Lady since the 12th century. They are the Prophesy of Simeon (Lk 2:34-35), the flight into Egypt (Mt 2:13), the loss of the Child Jesus in the temple (Lk 2:45-46), the way of the cross, the crucifixion, the descent from the cross, and the burial of the Body of Jesus (Lk 23:26-56).

The month of **October** comes from the Latin word octo which is eight. October was the eighth month of the ancient Roman calendar.

In 1571, Pope Pius V, during the strategic naval Battle of Lapento, called on the sailors and all Christians to pray the Rosary. The Pope attributed the victory to Our Lady's intercession and named October 7th the feast day of Our Lady of Victory which later became known as Our Lady of the Rosary.

Catholics dedicate October to the Holy Rosary.

November gets its name from the Latin word novem which is nine. It was the ninth month in the ancient Roman calendar.

Catholics dedicated November to the souls in Purgatory, a place between heaven and earth where departed souls remain until they are purified from their sins.

December, the tenth month in the ancient Roman Calendar, gets its name from decem which is ten.

Catholics dedicate December to the Immaculate Conception, the fact that Mary was conceived and born free from original sin. At Lourdes, France in 1858, Mary appeared to Bernadette Soubirous and said, "I am the Immaculate Conception."

Gregorian Calendar: 178

JULIAN 1582		October			Gregorian 1582	
Sun	Mon	Tues	Wed	Thurs	Fri	Sat
	1	2	3	4	15	16
17	18	19	20	21	22	23
24	25	26	27	28	29	30
31						

Julius Caesar promulgated a calendar in 46 B.C. By the late 15th century, it was 10 days out of step with the seasons. Pope Gregory XIII put together a team of scholars under the leadership of the German Jesuit mathematician and astrologer, Christopher Clavius, to correct the error. As a result of the work of this team, Pope Gregory, in 1582, issued a decree that October 5th, 1582, would be October 15th, 1582. He also added a leap year every four years. The Gregorian calendar is considered accurate to within one day in 20,000 years. Most of Europe adopted this calendar quickly. Some of the Orthodox churches still adhere to the Julian calendar which is now 13 days off.

Jubilee Year: 179

A Jubilee year is a special year of remission of sins and universal pardon. Pope Boniface VIII established the first Jubilee Year in 1300 A. D. Popes, since then, have proclaimed Jubilee years during which pilgrims who come to Rome can gain a Plenary Indulgence under the usual conditions. This custom comes from the Old Testament time when, every fifty years, debts were canceled. In 1470, Pope Paul II, decreed Jubilee years take place every 25 years. The most recent one was in the year 2000 when millions went to Rome and millions more went to designated churches in their home diocese in order to gain the Plenary Indulgence for the reduction or removal of the punishment due to our sins.

PRAYERS

The Our Father: 180

Some Christians end the Our Father with a doxology, a beautiful hymn of praise to God. It says, "For thine is the kingdom and the power and the glory for ever and ever. Amen." What is the origin of this doxology?

It was originally put in the margin of the biblical text by a monk as he was copying the Bible by hand, the way they copied the Bible until the printing press. The Eastern Church used the phrase for centuries. The majority of Greek transcripts from the 5th to the 12th centuries contain this doxology.

The Lord did not compose the Our Father with this ending. The Gospels of Matthew and Luke do not have this ending. Also, the doxology is not an accurate representation of Jesus' words, and, after all, we do say in the Mass that we pray, "with confidence to the Father in the words Our Savior gave us."

The Hail Mary: 181

The Archangel Gabriel saluted Mary as *full of grace* when he appeared to her at Nazareth. The Hail Mary, as we pray it today, is the result of a gradual development from the 6th to the 16th centuries, when the present wording was adopted. In its present form, the Hail Mary received official recognition by the Church when Pope Pius V included it in the *Roman Breviary* of 1568.

The Hail Mary can be divided into three parts:

First, from Lk 1:28-30, Hail, full of grace. The Lord is with you. Blessed are you among women. These are the words of the Archangel Gabriel to Mary when he announced the request of God that she become the mother of His Son. The name Mary was added around the 13th century.

Second, after the Archangel Gabriel came to Mary, she went into the hill country to a town of Judah, where she greeted her cousin Elizabeth. Elizabeth said to Mary that she is blest among women, and blest is the fruit of your womb (Lk 1:42). The name of Jesus was added in the Middle Ages, probably due to the initiative of Pope Urban IV in 1261.

Third, the petition is "Holy Mary, Mother of God, pray for us sinners, now, and at the hour of our death. Amen." This part developed in the 14th century during and after the Black Plague that raged through Europe. In the 16th century, it was approved by the Church itself and officially recognized in the Roman Breviary of 1568. So, the first part of

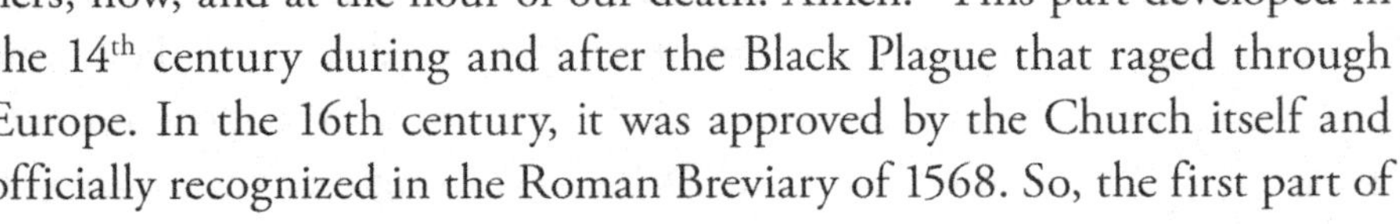

the Hail Mary is from the Bible, and in the second part we ask Mary to pray for us now and when we are dying.

The Rosary:

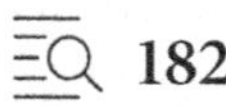 **182**

The Rosary is a very popular prayer in the Catholic Church. The word rosary comes from the Latin word rosarium which is a rose garden. In this case, it is a garland or circular arrangement of materials, such as flowers, which are attached to each other. Here, it is the flowers of the Hail Marys which are attached to each other.

The rose is one of the flowers which is used to symbolize the Blessed Virgin Mary. In Lk 1:42, Elizabeth said to Mary, "Blessed are you among women." Even earlier, in Lk 1:28, the Angel Gabriel said, "Hail, Full of Grace." Devotion to Our Lady is older than the Church. Not until the Middle Ages were these two greetings used as prayers. During the Middle Ages, devotion to Mary was strong. People would say Ave or Hail many times a day. From this repetition, the Rosary developed.

During the Middle Ages, a great prayer of the Church was the Divine Office, or as we name it today, the Liturgy of the Hours. All over Europe, priests and monks stopped their work seven times a day to chant the Psalms and hymns from the Divine Office. The bells called the monks and priests to prayer. The people heard the bells and wanted to join them in prayer, but they were not able to do so, since they could not read or write.

In about the year 800 A.D., an Irish monk put forth the idea that the people could pray the Our Father instead of the Psalms. This became popular and before long this practice spread throughout Europe. There was, however, a problem. The monks chanted 150 Psalms. The people had trouble keeping track of 150 Our Fathers as to how many were said and how many had still to be said. They began to wear little pouches on their belts. In these pouches, they had 150 stones. Some carried ropes with 50 to 150 knots on them. The way of counting improved, until eventually, Catholics carried strings with 50 prayer beads and a cross. The word bead comes from the Old English gebed, which means prayer.

They prayed the Our Father on each bead called a Paternoster, a name derived from the Latin for Our Father.

The Marian devotion followed a similar trend. In the 11th century, St. Peter Damien wrote about using these beads to count out Aves or Hails, the salutation of the Archangel Gabriel, instead of the Our Fathers. The practice was probably popular before he wrote this, which is the oldest record we have of counting Aves on the beads instead of the Our Fathers. By the 12th century, this was the custom, and even in the 14th century, the beads were still called the Paternosters, even though they were used to count the Aves or Hails.

As time went on, other traditions evolved. The people liked to say the words of 150 Pater Nosters (Our Fathers) or Aves and then meditate on some events in the lives of Jesus or Mary. Eventually, these four ways of praying, saying the Our Fathers, Hail Marys, meditating on the lives of Jesus, or of Mary, came together to form the Rosary as we know it today. It took a long, long time.

In 1365, a Carthusian monk, Henry of Kalkar, divided the 50 Aves into 5 groups of 10, and each group was preceded by an Our Father. In 1409, another Carthusian monk, Dominic the Prussian, wrote a book giving 50 thoughts about Jesus and Mary for the 50 Hail Mary beads. This was called the Rosarium, it became popular, and the two ideas were combined. Each group of 10 Hail Marys became a decade, and during the time a person was saying the decade, he or she would concentrate on an event in the life of Jesus or Mary. In 1480, the 50 thoughts were reduced to five, one for each decade. The Dominican, Alberto da Castello, in 1521, used the word mystery when referring to the thoughts a person meditates on as he or she says the decade, or 10 Hail Marys. Finally, what we call the Rosary today was formed.

In the early 1200's according to tradition, Our Lady appeared to St. Dominic and told him to promote the Rosary. The Dominicans saw the Rosary as an ideal way to teach the faith, so they preached the Rosary wherever they went. The Glory Be, namely, "Glory be to the Father and to the Son, and to the Holy Spirit as it was in the beginning is now and ever shall be, world without end. Amen." was added in the 15th century. In 1569, Pope Pius V officially approved the Rosary in the form of the 15 decades, each introduced by the Our Father followed by 10 Hail Marys and each decade concluded with the Glory Be.

Using beads to count prayers is not confined to the Catholic Church. Ancient evidence of prayer beads was found among the Hindus in India. The prayer beads were adopted by the Buddhists in Tibet, China and Japan. Muslims use a misbaha of 99 beads plus one to recite the 3 praises of Allah, 33 times for each name. Praying the Rosary is not confined to the Catholic Church. Many other Christians pray the Rosary as well, especially Episcopalians, some Anglicans and Lutherans.

The Angelus:

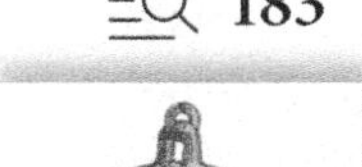

Angelus is the Latin word meaning Angel. The prayer begins with "The Angel of the Lord declared unto Mary". Three Hail Marys and other short prayers bring to mind the mystery of the Incarnation, or God becoming man. It is said three times each day: at 6am, noon, and 6pm. A bell is rung at these times. Praying three times each day came into being gradually. The ringing of the evening bell to announce curfew and the ringing of the evening bell to announce the Angelus do not seem to be connected.

In the 11th century, Pope Gregory IX is said to have promoted the daily ringing of the evening bell to remind the faithful to pray for the crusades. In 1269, St. Bonaventure told his fellow Franciscans to encourage the faithful to pray three Hail Marys when the bell rang in the evening. The morning Angelus seems to have come from a 14th century custom of praying three Hail Marys at the sound of the bell during Prime, which is early morning prayer of the Liturgy of the Hours, the official prayer of the Church. The noon Angelus came from a devotion to the Passion or suffering of Christ. During this devotion a bell was rung at noon on Fridays. Prayers for peace were offered at this time also. This practice was first mentioned by the Synod of Prague in 1386 and was extended to the whole Church when Pope Callistus III, in 1456, asked everyone to pray for victory over the Turks. These three customs were joined together in the 16th century, and that is how we got the Angelus.

Litany: 184

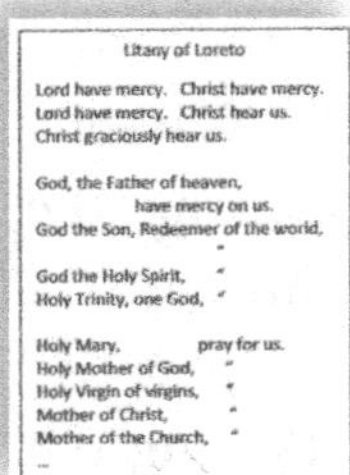
Litany of Loreto

Lord have mercy. Christ have mercy.
Lord have mercy. Christ hear us.
Christ graciously hear us.

God, the Father of heaven,
have mercy on us.
God the Son, Redeemer of the world,
"

God the Holy Spirit, "
Holy Trinity, one God, "

Holy Mary, pray for us.
Holy Mother of God, "
Holy Virgin of virgins, "
Mother of Christ, "
Mother of the Church, "
...

The litany, the form of prayer which follows a uniform rhythm of a call and a response, goes back at least to the time of King David (1000 B.C.). His Psalm 136 is written this way. Both the pagans and the Christians in ancient times used this form while walking in procession. The pagans used it when installing their emperors, and the Christians of Rome while assembling for Sunday Mass.

The Litany of Our Lady of Loreto is popular. Medieval Loreto, Italy was a famous shrine of the Blessed Virgin and the litany as we have it now was recited there by pilgrims from all over Europe. It was composed about the end of the 15th century when printing was available. Some titles given to Our Lady sound as if they come from Scripture. They do have a background in Scripture but are taken from various medieval poems written in praise of Mary.

There are only six litanies approved by the Church. They are the Litany of the Holy Name of Jesus, Litany of the Sacred Heart of Jesus, Litany of the Precious Blood of Jesus, Litany of Our Lady of Loreto or the Blessed Virgin Mary, Litany of St. Joseph and Litany of the Saints.

The Stations of the Cross: 185

In the ancient world, non-Christians often visited places which were sacred to them. Christians did the same. There is a legend which says that the Blessed Virgin Mary often visited places which were sacred to the early Christians, especially places where her Son, Jesus, suffered, and they stop to pray and meditate at those places. A favorite place for them to go to pray and meditate was from the Roman courtyard, where Pilot condemned Jesus to death, and along the journey to Calvary, called the Way of the Cross. Jesus had to carry His cross to Calvary, where He was crucified.

Events happened which made it difficult for them to do these sacred walks. The first was the destruction of Jerusalem by the Romans in 70 A.D., and also the continued persecution of the Christians by the

Romans until the 4th century when the Emperor, Constantine, decreed that Christianity could be practiced openly.

St. Jerome (342-420), who translated the Bible called the *Vulgate,* described pilgrimages throughout the Holy Land and said that the most popular one was along the road which Jesus traveled from Pilate's Courtyard to Calvary. Along this road there are places where people can stop and meditate on what happened at that particular place. These stopping places are now called stations from the Latin word stare, which is to stop. In our own times we have stations, or stopping places, too, like gas stations, weigh stations, visitor's centers and so on.

The first set of Stations of the Cross outside of Palestine was set up in the Church of San Stefano in Bologna, Italy in the 5th century. Pilgrims from all over Europe would go to the Holy Land to visit the sacred sites. However, another problem arose when the Muslims took over the Holy Land (636-637). Then, for centuries it was dangerous for Christians to visit these holy places. Crusaders took back the Holy Land, and they saw how the pilgrims would visit the holy places and travel the Way of the Cross or make the Stations of the Cross. When the Crusaders returned home, they set up Stations of the Cross where people who could not go to the Holy Land could go and pray the Way of the Cross.

The idea of having shrines to bring to mind the suffering and death of Jesus Christ became popular. So, in the 14th century, Blessed Alvarez of Cordova, a Dominican, made sets of shrines in Cordova, Spain similar to the Stations of the Cross. In 1217, St. Francis of Assisi founded *Custody of the Holy Land.* In 1342, Pope Clement VI granted the Franciscans the task of guarding the holy places in the Holy Land. The Franciscans promoted the passion or suffering of Christ, and that included the Stations of the Cross. Gradually the Stations of the Cross became more popular. They were first set up in Franciscan churches only. Later, in 1731, Pope Clement XII extended it to all parishes throughout the world. One Franciscan, St. Leonard of Port Maurice, was known as the Preacher of the Way of the Cross because he is said to have set up over 570 sets of the Way of the Cross or Stations of the Cross.

At first there was no set number of stations. There could be as many as 30. William Wey, an English pilgrim, was the first to call these stopping places Stations. He visited the Holy Land in 1458 & 1462. The writer, Adrichomius, in his book about Jerusalem in 1584, came up with the number 12, and these 12 are the same as the first 12 Stations of the Cross, which we have today. The number 14 and the method of praying at those stations took shape during the 16th century.

Pope Clement XII fixed the number of stations at 14 in 1731. Usually there are 14 icons (images) or 14 sets of statues to help to remind one of the particular events in Christ's passion being meditated upon. However, we must remember that neither the icons nor the statues are the stations. The cross is the essential element present on each of these stations. There are no set required prayers to be said at each station, only the requirement that one meditate on the sufferings of Christ and what they mean to us.

Today, we have booklets with the images of the events of each station and prayers to go along with them. A crossbearer, accompanied by two candle bearers, can move along the stations and stand in front of the station while the prayers and singing are done.

The 14 Stations of the Cross are: (1) Jesus is condemned to death, (2) Jesus is made to bear his cross, (3) Jesus falls the first time, (4) Jesus meets his mother, (5) Simon of Cyrene is made to bear the cross, (6) Veronica wipes Jesus' face, (7) Jesus falls the second time, (8) The women of Jerusalem weep over Jesus, (9) Jesus falls the third time, (10) Jesus is stripped of his garments, (11) Jesus is nailed to the cross, (12) Jesus dies on the cross, (13) Jesus is taken down from the cross, and (14) Jesus is placed in the sepulcher.

The images are usually mounted on the inside walls of churches, chapels, cemeteries, corridors of hospitals and religious houses, or on mountainsides.

Alleluia or Hallelujah:

This is a Hebrew word which means, Praise the Lord, or Praise Yahweh, or Glory to Him Who Is. It is an expression of praise and joy which is found in the Psalms (Psalms 104-106, 135) and sung by the choirs in heaven (Rev. 19:1-6). It was introduced into the official prayer of the Church (Liturgy) in the early centuries and is popular today.

Amen:

This is a Hebrew word which means certainly, or it is true, or so be it. It is often used to mark the end of a prayer as an expression of agreement.

Glory:

It is the praise belonging to someone on account of his excellence. It is also praise given to God in recognition of His Might and Perfection. In the Old Testament, God's Glory is shown in a cloud, in light, in fire or in smoke. In Ex 13:21-22, we have the example of the pillar of cloud and the pillar of fire.

Pilgrimage:

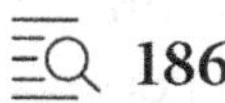 **186**

To make a pilgrimage is to travel to a holy place in order to obtain some spiritual benefit. The person who travels for this purpose is called a pilgrim. The reason why a person goes on a pilgrimage could be to venerate a sacred object or relic, to be in the presence of a holy person, to do penance, to seek a favor, or to offer thanks for graces received. In the Old Testament, there were also pilgrimages. The Ark of the Covenant was taken on pilgrimage to Jerusalem by David and his men (2 Samuel 6).

Man has always had the desire to visit sacred places. He would journey to mountains, lakes and rivers where he believed gods lived. The pilgrim impulse stirred in the early Christians also. They went on pilgrimage to the Holy Land, to Rome and to Mount Gargano in South Italy where St. Michael appeared. Clerics planned the routes to take, the places to stay, the guides to get, etc., much as it is today. On account of the persecutions during the first 300 years, the pilgrimages to Rome were dangerous. But people continued to go on pilgrimage. The medieval pilgrim was spurred on by piety, but not everyone was of the same mind, and the spirit of the world crept into the pilgrimages.

An 8th century poet said, "To go to Rome means great labor and little profit; the king you seek can only be found there if you bring him within you." In the 9th century, a new place of pilgrimage arose, Compostela in Spain where it was said that the relics of St. James were discovered. The

House of Loreto was another popular place of pilgrimage. Tradition said that in 1291 angels carried the house of the Holy Family from Nazareth to a town on the Adriatic Coast of Italy, now Ancone. The little stone house can be seen today inside the Basilica della Santa Casa or Basilica of the Holy House in Loreto, Spain. Fifty popes have honored this shrine.

The most severe place of pilgrimage in Christianity is in Lough Derg in County Donegal, Ireland. It is the Sanctuary of St. Patrick and is an extremely popular place of pilgrimage today. The three-day pilgrimage is not for the faint hearted. The most popular place of pilgrimage in the New World is the Shrine of Our Lady of Guadalupe, near Mexico City. In Europe popular places of pilgrimage are Lourdes in France, Fatima in Portugal, Knock in Ireland, Garabandal in Spain and Medjugorje in Bosnia-Herzegovina.

Novena:

187

The word novena comes from the Latin word novem meaning nine. So, a novena is nine consecutive days of private or public prayer to obtain special favors or graces. Many say that the first novena was the nine days which the Apostles spent in Jerusalem praying and waiting for the Holy Spirit to come, as the Lord had promised.

However, before this, the novena was first introduced as a period of mourning. The Greeks, Romans and other ancient peoples were accustomed to observing nine days of mourning. A special feast was held on the 9th day after the death or burial. In Jewish customs, the Nine Days of Av is communal and personal mourning for the tragedies of the Jewish people. Since early Christianity, there has been the custom of praying novenas. In the Middle Ages, the custom was having a novena of prayer in preparation for some special occasion. Also, novenas became popular in seeking the intercession of Our Lady or the saints for some favor or blessing, like a healing. A novena is very good. It can be very helpful in learning perseverance in prayer.

PART SIX

ONE OF THE GREATEST

OF THE SIGNS AND SYMBOLS

OUR LADY OF GUADALUPE 188

There are many signs or symbols in the Catholic Church, but one that has produced the most profound change on a nation and on people in general is the image of Our Lady of Guadalupe and the symbols on the image.

On Dec. 9th, 1531, Our Lady appeared to an Aztec Indian, named Juan Diego, outside of Mexico City. He was a convert to the Catholic faith and was on his way to Mass. Our Lady gave him messages, and the final message was imprinted on his tilma or cloak. The image is of Our Lady, herself, and there are several symbols on the cloak and on the whole image which provided a wealth of information to the Aztec wise men.

These symbols spoke volumes to the Aztec Indians, and they speak to us today.

THE STORY OF OUR LADY OF GUADALUPE

The story of Our Lady of Guadalupe begins way back between 590 and 604 when Pope Gregory the Great gave a statue of Our Lady to the Bishop of Seville, Spain. In 711, the Moslems were taking over Spain and setting up their laws. The Christians were retreating, and they put the statue of Our Lady in an iron casket, buried it and did not mark the spot.

Five hundred years later, in the 1200's, Our Lady appeared to a man who was looking after cattle. She showed him where the statue was buried in the little village of Guadalupe, Spain. The statue was dug up and a shrine was built. The shrine became popular for hundreds of years. Kings, queens, and regular people went there. Queen Isabelle went there. Christopher Columbus, before he set out on his voyage towards the west in 1492, prayed there. So, the Shrine of Our Lady of Guadalupe in Spain was very popular.

THE AZTEC INDIANS IN MEXICO

The Aztecs had a very advanced civilization. Their legal system was like ours. All major crimes against society were punishable by death. Stealing was punishable by death. People were stoned to death for adultery.

The Aztecs could make hundreds of medicines from herbs and plants. They had hospitals and surgeons that the Spaniards considered to be as good as the surgeons in Europe.

They wrote on a fine grade of paper made from maguey cactus and were excellent at astronomy. They had many religious practices, which resembled religious practices in the Catholic Church. Right after birth they had a kind of infant baptism. Marriages were witnessed by their priests. Also, there was a type of confession, which took place when a person was old. It was celebrated only once in a lifetime and a person could never be punished by civil authorities for anything confessed in the confession. The priest gave the person a penance. They also had feast days, days of fast, processions and different services.

But the Aztecs practiced human sacrifice. They would attack other tribes, take prisoners, and sacrifice these prisoners by cutting out their hearts. It would take an Aztec priest only 15 seconds to perform this function. Well over 50,000 people were sacrificed each year, to appease their god, Quetzalcoatl, the feathered serpent. The victims were held down on a stone altar. Their chests were cut open. Their still beating hearts were ripped from their bodies and held aloft to their bloodthirsty god. It is estimated that 1 out of 5 children were sacrificed in Mexico. The Aztec culture was one of the most satanic in history. In 1487, only 44 years before Our Lady appeared to Juan Diego, the Aztecs sacrificed an estimated 80,400 human victims in four days to reconsecrate the Great Pyramid of Tenochtitlan.

Hernando Cortez arrived in Mexico in February 1519 with 11 ships, 600 men, 500 soldiers and 100 sailors, 16 horses, 10 to 14 cannons and several statues of Our Lady. They were up against 20 million Indians. Cortez defeated some Indian tribes, who were enemies of the Aztecs, enlisted their help and eventually defeated the Aztecs.

How could such a small force defeat a huge empire headed by Montezuma? Ten years before Cortez came to Mexico Montezuma's sister, Princess Papantzin, fell into a deep coma. The people, thinking she was dead, buried her in a tomb. While in the tomb, she had a powerful religious experience. She was guided by an angel to the shores of a vast ocean. She saw huge ships come into view. On their sails were black crosses. The angel had the same black cross on his forehead. He told her that these ships would bring men who would conquer all the land and bring knowledge of the One True God, Creator of heaven and earth. The princess herself would be one of the first to receive the waters that wash away sin.

The princess regained consciousness and cried out for help and the tomb was opened. She told her brother, Montezuma, and her whole court about her experiences. Ten years later the ships with the black crosses came. The leader was Hernando Cortez. This is one of the reasons why Montezuma surrendered so easily to the Spaniards.

By the end of 1531, the Spaniards had ruled over the Aztecs for 10 years. However, the Spanish leaders had become ruthless in their unquenchable thirst for wealth and power. The Aztecs realized that the Spaniards were not gods but only human beings like themselves. They became restless and did not take kindly to the religion the Spaniards were trying to spread. The Spaniards brought Franciscan and Dominican missionaries with them when they came to Mexico. These missionaries had to deal with the Spaniards' mistreatment of the Indians and with infighting between their religious communities. The result was that there were very few converts.

Bishop Zumarraga, bishop of the area, prayed to Our Lady for a solution to the threat posed by the Aztecs whom he sensed were ready to revolt and destroy the Spaniards. He asked Our Lady for a sign that she would intercede, and he specifically asked her to send him some Castilian roses. These roses had never before grown in Mexico, and it was not a well-known flower.

On December 9, 1531, an Indian named Juan Diego was passing the Hill of Tepeyac near Mexico City, on his way to Mass. He was baptized about 5 years earlier and walked the 8 miles to Mass on Saturday and Sunday mornings. The temperatures in the early morning were very cold. Suddenly Juan heard birds singing and beautiful music. He stopped and saw a heaven and earth.

A beautiful lady appeared to him. She said, "It is my earnest wish that a temple be built here to my honor. Here I will demonstrate, I will exhibit, I will give all my love, my compassion, my help, and my protection to the people. I am your merciful mother, the merciful mother of all of you who live united in this land, and of all mankind, of all those who love me, of those who cry to me, of those who seek me, of those who have confidence in me. Here, I will hear their weeping, their sorrow, and will remedy and alleviate all their multiple sufferings, necessities, and misfortunes. Do not be troubled. Are you not under my shadow, my protection? Am I not here who am your mother? Are you not in the folds of my mantle? In the crossing of my arms? Is there anything else you need?"

Our Lady said that she wished for a church to be built in that place where she will be honored, and she asked Juan Diego to go to the bishop and arrange it. The bishop doubted Juan Diego's story, so he asked him to bring a sign as a proof that Our Lady appeared to him. When Juan Diego told Our Lady that the bishop wanted a sign, she said to him, "Go to the top of the hill and there you will find some flowers. I ask you to pick them." It was not the season for delicate flowers, especially on the Hill of Tepeyac, which is a desert. But he went as he was told and found a whole host of Castilian roses growing there. He picked the roses, Our Lady arranged them in his cloak (tilma) and off he went to the bishop. He opened his cloak and the roses fell to the floor. The bishop and those present looked in shock, not at the roses, but at the image of Our Lady on the cloak.

Our Lady also appeared to Juan Bernardino, Juan Diego's uncle, who was ill. She told him that he would be healed and that she would be known as the ever-virgin Holy Mary of Guadalupe. Bishop Zumarraga was already familiar with the Shrine of Guadalupe in Spain.

Today, the tilma is 60" (170 cm) high and 41" (105 cm) wide and is under bullet proof glass. The tilma can be seen in the Basilica in Guadalupe north of Mexico City near the hill of Tepeyac.

This event caused the greatest conversion story the world has ever seen.

In 7 years over 8 million Aztecs were baptized.

And human sacrifice was stopped.

Today, this is the greatest shrine in honor of Our Lady in the whole world. Twenty million people visit there each year.

THE TILMA

189

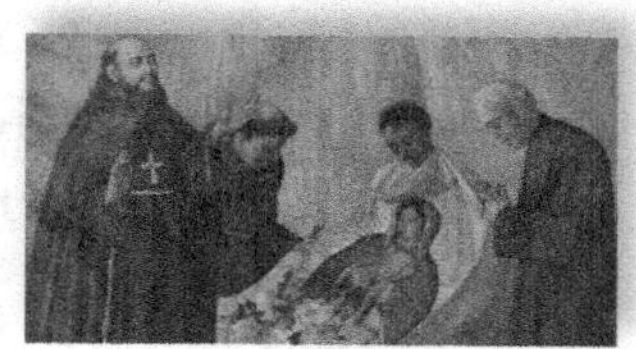

The tilma was a sign of one's status in the community. Only the nobility could put color and decoration on their clothing. Juan Diego was an ordinary man. Therefore, his clothes were the original color of the material from which they were made.

When Our Lady put her likeness on the tilma of Juan Diego in the colors of an empress, she was acknowledging his dignity and the dignity of all the Indian peoples.

In Juan Diego's day the tilma was used for many reasons, for work, for travel, to carry supplies from the farm and market and to keep oneself warm. By putting her image on the tilma, Mary was placing herself in a close relationship with the Indian people and their culture.

In his tilma, Juan Diego carried the flowers to the bishop. When he opened the tilma to drop the flowers on the floor, the image of Our Lady is imprinted on the tilma.

The tilma is made of ayate fiber which is derived from the maguey cactus plant. It is made of two pieces. A seam runs down the middle which makes it a poor material on which to paint. There are defects in it, but each defect is in the right place. Normally, the life span of this type of garment is about 20-30 years. Science cannot explain how it has lasted almost 500 years. It was left completely unprotected for 116 years. There was no glass in front of it. It was exposed to the dreadful climate, to strong nitrous fumes given off by Lake Texcoco, humidity, smoke and heat from candles that burned at all hours, people touching it with their hands, rosaries, medals, lips, swords, etc. The fiber absorbed a lot of moisture, and insects attacked it. Yet, after almost 500 years the tilma is in as good a condition as it was in 1531.

The valleys, around the former Lake Texcoco, have a mild climate and are rich in salt. The air is full of salt particles. All of these things added together give rise to buildings falling apart and the rusting of iron. But the tilma lives on.

The colors seem to be faded when looked at through a magnifying glass. However, they are fresh and vigorous when seen from a distance. When one is close to the tilma, the color of the mantle is dark blue. From a distance, it is blue green. When one is close to the tilma, the stars on her robe can scarcely be seen. Yet they can be clearly seen when looked at from a distance. There are no brush strokes. The image was created on the tilma in one instant. There is no protective coating on the tilma.

The Image:

This image is a story in pictures. It tells part of the message that Our Lady brought through Juan Diego to the Indians of Mexico and to all the peoples of the Americas. Every detail in the image is symbolic. The symbols had a special meaning to the Indians who, because of their culture, could decipher the code in the Image.

The Spaniards saw a maiden standing on a black moon. To them it was an image of the Assumption of Our Lady into heaven. However, the Indian wise men saw much more. They saw the deep meaning of every symbol. They saw several meanings in their symbols just as we can see several meanings in our symbols. They explained the symbols to Bishop Zumarraga.

The overwhelming meaning of the image for the Indians was LIFE, motherhood, evangelization and bringing people together in peace. The image is an emblem of the people just as the eagle in the shield of the Mexican flag is a symbol for the city of Tenochtitlan, now Mexico City, the center of the Aztec Empire. This recalls the legend of the eagle, sitting on a cactus devouring a serpent, that was a signal to the Aztec where to found their city, Tenochtitlan.

The image of Our Lady of Guadalupe, along with the Shroud of Turin, the burial cloth of Jesus Christ with His image imprinted on it, have possibly become the most mysterious images on earth.

Pictures:

In Aztec culture pictures were a necessary means of communication. The tilma was a perfect means. It is a codex or record composed of images which are imprinted on paper made from maguey fibers. The wise men knew how to read and interpret the ideas that Our Lady was revealing to them in the image. They would read the tilma from different angles. They were amazed at how the Catholic faith was explained to them in a way that they could understand.

The Position of the Body:

Our Lady's right foot is on the moon and the other foot is flexed as in a dance step. The people understood that she is dancing. For the native people, dance was the same as prayer.

Her left knee is bent. Mary is taking a step as if dancing or walking. Her body is delicately balanced, and her hands are situated to suggest that she is holding something.

The Virgin addressed the Indian, Juan Diego, as a person, a man, and that is why she appeared to him in a standing position. Conquerors, whoever they may be, whether Aztec, Mayan, Incas or Spaniards were always seated when they received inferiors. Juan Diego sees nobility in the Lady and not domination.

Mary's Mantle:

190

The mantle represents the sky or the heavens above us. It is wrapped around her shoulders and circles around her dress, which symbolizes the earth. Heaven and earth come together in this way. In 1983 it was found that the stars on Mary's mantle are the same ones present over Mexico City just before sunrise on December 12, 1531, the morning of the winter solstice.

The mantle is blue green in color. Only an emperor could wear that color. It signifies that she is an empress. Blue symbolized the sky, and green symbolized earth and life.

The Dress:

191

The dress is a pale red color, the color of the blood which was spilled in the sacrifices. It was also the color of dawn in the Valley of Mexico. The dress represents earth. The dress has flowers imprinted upon it. The flowers are symbols of truth. The Aztec wise men looked upon flowers and song as the only truth on earth.

The dress is pale pink when seen close-up, but light red when seen from a distance.

Flowers:

Our Lady sent flowers to Bishop Zumarraga as a sign to him that the apparitions were true. The Aztecs used flowers to convey the message that their messages were true. The flowers on Our Lady's dress convey the message that her message is true. The leaf and flower design symbolizes heaven which she enjoys and wants us to enjoy also.

The Nahuatl wise men looked upon flowers as a symbol of truth. They were the loveliest things they knew. The native messengers of their ancestors always accompanied their messages with flowers as a symbol of truth.

The 4 Petal Flower:

193

This four petal Jasmine flower is over the Virgin's womb in an X position. It is the most important symbol in the image and the only one of its design among the fifty-seven flowers and thirteen buds on Our Lady's dress. The Aztecs recognized it immediately. It is called the Flower of the Sun. It is in the center of the Aztec Calendar. This announced to the conquered Indians that the Sun of a new era was about to be born in their lives. It symbolized new life for a people who were on the edge of total despair as a result of:

The conquest,

The loss of their gods. They felt their gods betrayed them in spite of all the human sacrifices offered to them,

The loss of their culture and temples,

The loss of their freedom,

The loss of their family and friends with smallpox,

The loss of their self-worth.

The Sun of a New Era is about to be born. The four-petal flower on Mary's womb announced to the Indians that the apparitions and all connected with them were true. In the thinking of the native people at that time, this tiny flower, with its 4 petals, was a representation of the dwelling place of God. She is God's Mother and is about to give birth to Him. This is the most important codex in the entire image. For the Aztecs, the image proclaimed that the Most Holy Virgin carries within herself the Sun, that is, God.

Face:

194

For the Aztecs the face indicated what a person was like. It was a window to the inner person. It was a means by which one could read who a person was and the way that person would act. Mary's face shows humility, compassion, understanding, assurance of protection, sweetness and modesty.

Her face shows her with dark skin and dark hair like the Indians themselves. So, she is one of them. She also spoke in their language which was Nahuatl. Also, her complexion represents the union of two races, the Indian and the European. These two mighty empires had lived as enemies, but now they are joined together to form a new people, the Mexican people.

She has the features of an Aztec maiden which identifies her with the conquered and enslaved Indians. The Indians needed someone of their own race, culture and mentality to teach the Catholic faith to them. She, more than anyone else showed the Aztecs the way to the true God. The Spaniards had brutally blocked that way. Mary chose Juan Diego as the Indian's representative and by doing this she was honoring his dignity and the dignity of his people.

195

Eyes:

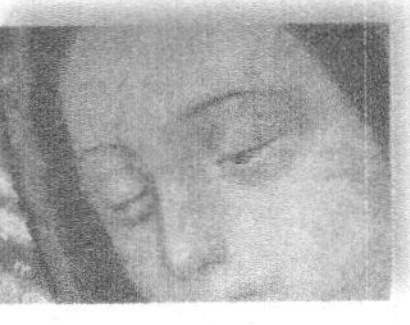

Mary's eyes are looking down. This is a position of humility. It is a symbol that said to the Indians that, as great as she is, she is not a goddess. Indian gods never looked down. They looked straight ahead. She is not proud. In the cornea of Our Lady's eyes, there are thirteen people reflected in the eyes. It would be impossible to paint these reflections in the eyes given such little space.

In 1956 ophthalmologist Dr. Rafael Torrija Lavoignet examined the eyes of Mary in the image with an ophthalmoscope and observed a human figure in the corneas of both eyes in the location and distortion of a normal human eye. The unique appearance of the eyes looked strangely "alive" when examined. Earlier that same year ophthalmologist Dr. Javier Torroella Bueno certified that the images in the eyes are located where they would be in a living human eye, and that the distortion of the images agree with the curvature of the cornea.

In 1979, Dr. Jose Aste Tonsmann magnified the image of the tilma 2,500 times with digitized high-resolution and discovered thirteen human figures reflected in the eyes. The same people are present in both the left and right eyes, in different proportions, as would happen when human eyes reflect the objects before them.

Dr. Tonsmann said he believes the reflection transmitted by the eyes is the scene on Dec. 12, 1531, during which Juan Diego opened his tilma to Bishop Juan de Zumarraga and the others present in the room. Nuclear physicist Dr. Charles Wahlig also figured that the Blessed Mother must have been standing there in the room invisibly present when Juan Diego was presenting the roses to Bishop Zumarraga and that the tilma acted like a photographic plate that captured her image and the reflection of their images in her eyes.

In the eyes, Dr. Tonsmann found a seated Indian, who is looking up to the heavens; the profile of a balding, elderly man with a white beard, much like the portrait of Bishop Zumarraga painted later by Miguel Cabrera to depict the miracle; a younger man, probably interpreter Juan González; an Indian with a beard and mustache, likely Saint Juan Diego who unfolds his own tilma before the bishop; a woman of dark complexion, possibly a Negro slave who was in the bishop's service; and a man with Spanish features who looks on while stroking his beard with his hand.

There is another scene, independent of the first, in the center of the pupils, and in a much more reduced scale. It is an Indian family made up of a woman, a man, and several children. In the right eye, other people who are standing appear behind the woman.

Hands:

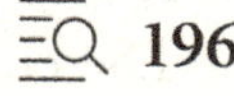 196

Mary's hands are joined together in a posture of prayer. The Spaniards recognized this. However, the Indians saw more in this posture of the hands. They also saw another posture which they had in prayer, and that was dance. The Indians expressed prayer not only by the hands, but also by the whole body.

Our Lady of Guadalupe is shown in a position of dancing prayer, with her left knee bent in movement. Above her hands and on her tunic, is one of the nine heart shaped flower blossoms. This is a symbol of love and sacrifice. Mary's heart is held between her hands in an act of prayer and offering to God.

The ancestors of the Indians, to keep harmony in their lives, offered hearts to their god after they tore them out of their victims. Mary is telling the people to place their own hearts in her hands, and she would present them to the true God without tearing them out.

Head:

197

Mary's head is bowed in reverence to Someone who is greater.

Hair:

In the Aztec culture, virgins wore their hair down. There was no braiding. Mary's long hair was neatly brushed.

Medallion: 198

Aztecs wore medallions around their necks. These medallions had a deep religious meaning for them. The Virgin had a medallion with a cross on it. This showed the Aztecs that she was a follower of Jesus Christ, her Son and True God. They had learned about the cross from the missionaries. The cross on the medallion was the same as the cross on the helmets of the Spanish soldiers. Therefore, she had the same religion as the Spaniards.

The cross and the four-petal flower indicate that Mary is both the bearer and a follower of Christ.

Dark Ribbon: 199

The dark ribbon worn above the waist signifies that Mary is with child. It was her child that she was offering to the New World and to all of the peoples of this New World.

Speech:

Our Lady speaks to Juan Diego in Nahuatl which was his language. He calls her, "My Lady", "My Queen", "My Little Girl", "My Child". She calls him, "My dear little one". Their conversation is the typical friendliness of the Nahuatl language.

Angel: 200

An angel is carrying Our Lady. In Aztec culture, only very important persons were carried on the shoulders of another. Only royalty and the representatives of the gods could be carried by others. The fact that she is carried by a heavenly creature meant that she came on her own, and not with the Spaniards, and also that she is a heavenly queen.

The face of the angel is that of an old man. This indicates the wisdom of the Indian wise men. The angel has Our Lady's mantle, signifying heaven, in his right hand and her dress, signifying earth, in his left hand. This indicates that heaven and earth are united. There will not be any war between them. It also represents a heavenly messenger because it was only the eagle which could fly high enough to give the hearts of those who were sacrificed to the sun god. The angel has eagle wings.

The purpose of the angel and also of evangelists, is to bring the divine and human together. In the Aztec way of thinking, if a human being had the wings of an angel, it meant that that person was reaching the heights of perfection. It was the eagle which showed the Aztecs where to settle down and build their civilization. For the Catholics the eagle represents John's Gospel.

The angel is seen as carrying in a new era or a new civilization. The old civilization had died, and Our Lady is bringing in a new one.

Moon:

 201

The Virgin stands in the center of the moon, or the center of Mexico. The word Mexico in Nahuatl is the navel of the moon. The moon is dark because the Virgin is eclipsing the sun. She is standing in front of the sun. The moon god, the god of night, was among the greatest of the Indian gods. The Virgin was standing upon the moon, so she is greater than the moon god.

Sun:

202

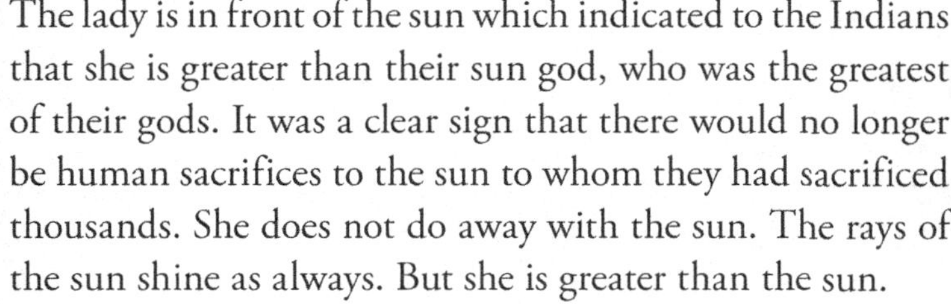

The lady is in front of the sun which indicated to the Indians that she is greater than their sun god, who was the greatest of their gods. It was a clear sign that there would no longer be human sacrifices to the sun to whom they had sacrificed thousands. She does not do away with the sun. The rays of the sun shine as always. But she is greater than the sun.

Stars:

203

In 1983 it was found that the stars on Mary's mantle are the same ones present over Mexico City just before sunrise on December 12, 1531, the morning of the winter solstice. The stars are in the position of the constellations that could be seen that morning. The number of stars on her mantle is 46. It is the same number of chromosomes, 23 pairs, which are in the human body and are in the child she is carrying.

ABOUT THE AUTHOR

John Noone was born in Ireland in December 1941. He grew up in Ireland with his family.

He was ordained on June 10, 1967 at St. Patrick's College, Carlow, Ireland and came to United States shortly after.

He received his Master's Degree in Social Work from Tulane University in New Orleans in 1971 and became a citizen of the United States in 1972.

He received the following appointments: 1967-1970 Assistant Pastor of Our Lady of the Gulf, Bay St. Louis, MS; 1970 Assistant Director of Catholic Charities; 1977 Director of Catholic Social Services for the newly established Diocese of Biloxi, MS; 1983 Pastor of three parishes – Holy Trinity in Columbia, MS, St. Paul in Tylertown, MS and St. Mary's Church, Sylvest, Ms; 1990 Pastor of St. Charles Borromeo in Picayune, MS; 2002 Pastor of Annunciation Church in Kiln, MS; 2014 Retired.

He continues working on his calling to get the truth out to all who are looking for it.

Fr. John Noone has compiled information for several CDs and books through the years of his priesthood from various sources and from his parishioners.

Fr. John Noone's Books can be found on
https://frjohnnoonesbooks.wordpress.com/

APPENDIX

For more information visit:
https://www.catholic.org/ Catholic Online World's Catholic Library
https://www.newadvent.org/ News, Encyclopedia, Summa, Bible, Library
https://www.franciscanmedia.org/ Resources, Saints, and more
https://scborromeo2.org/ St. Charles Borromeo Catholic Church – Complete Catechism of the Catholic Church with Table of Contents and indexes linking to the paragraphs, Bible Studies, Resources, and more

Sources of Images

001-Triangle	https://www.publicdomainpictures.net/en/view-image.php?image=30952&picture=basic-triangle-outline
002-Shamrock	https://publicdomainvectors.org/en/free-clipart/Three-leaves-clover/75323.html
003-Circle	https://www.publicdomainpictures.net/en/view-image.php?image=30947&picture=basic-circle-outline
004-Three Circles	https://publicdomainvectors.org/en/free-clipart/Trinity-symbols/53521.html
005-Triquetra	https://publicdomainvectors.org/en/free-clipart/Triquetra-drawing/31952.html
006-Hand of God	http://www.gocek.net/christiansymbols/images/hand-ofgod2.gif
007-Eye of God	https://commons.wikimedia.org/wiki/File:ChristianEyeOfProvidence.png
008-INRI	http://www.gocek.org/christiansymbols/images/inri.gif
009-ihs	https://commons.wikimedia.org/wiki/File:IHS-monogram-Jesus-medievalesque.svg
010-Chi Rho	https://en.wikipedia.org/wiki/Christogram#/media/File:Simple_Labarum.svg
011-Alpha&Omega	No results on Tineye or Google Search
012-Lamb	https://commons.wikimedia.org/wiki/File:Complete_Guide_to_Heraldry_Fig398.png

013-Good Shepherd	https://publicdomainvectors.org/en/free-clipart/Jesus-Christ-The-Shepherd/43902.html
014-Fish	https://publicdomainvectors.org/en/free-clipart/Sign-of-the-fish-vector/3380.html
015-Standard Bearer	Drawn by cvs - top part drawn using as a model https://www.clker.com/clipart-508706.html
016-King Crown	https://publicdomainvectors.org/en/free-clipart/Crown-monochrome-art/82729.html
017- Heart	https://en.wikipedia.org/wiki/Sacred_Heart#/media/File:Sagrado_Cora%C3%A7%C3%A3o_de_Jesus_-_escola_portuguesa,_s%C3%A9culo_XIX.png
018-Scepter	No results on tineye or google
019-Vine	https://publicdomainvectors.org/en/free-clipart/Grapes-illustration/62873.html
020-Dove	Drawn by cvs
021-Wind	Drawn by cvs
022-Fire	Drawn by cvs
023-Mt	https://www.fromoldbooks.org/Rossetti-Dante-LaVitaNuova/pages/120-detail-matthew-the-evangelist-angel/
024-Mk	https://www.fromoldbooks.org/Rossetti-Dante-LaVitaNuova/pages/120-detail-mark-the-evangelist-lion/#details
025-Lk	https://www.fromoldbooks.org/Rossetti-Dante-LaVitaNuova/pages/120-detail-luke-the-evangelist-ox/
026-Jn	https://www.fromoldbooks.org/Rossetti-Dante-LaVitaNuova/pages/120-detail-john-the-evangelist-eagle/
027-Pelican	http://www.gocek.com/christiansymbols/images/pelican.gif
028-Phoenix	gocek.org/christiansymbols/?search=animal
029-Peacock	http://www.gocek.org/christiansymbols/images/peacock.gif
030-Dove Peace	https://pixabay.com/vectors/dove-russula-sprig-oilseeds-bird-2798605/
031-Palm	https://pixy.org/475511/

032-Holy Water	Drawn by cvs
033-Salt	Drawn by cvs
034-Oil	http://www.clker.com/clipart-161957.html
035-Ashes	Drawn by cvs
036-Incense	With Permission https://www.smp.org/resourcecenter/resource/1620/
037-Medals	Camera shot of the medal
038-Scapulars	Picture of cvs' scapular
039-Holy Cards	http://www.marysrosaries.com/collaboration/index.php?title=File:Saint_Elisabeth_of_Hungary_with_roses.jpg
040-Bells	https://pixabay.com/vectors/bell-church-school-wedding-36238/ pixabay.com>vectors>bells
041-Big Candle	https://publicdomainvectors.org/en/free-clipart/Paschal-candle-symbols-for-2015-vector-clip-art/33255.html
042-Candles	Pixabay.com >vectors >candles Name: book-candle-desk-top-handdrawn-2497249
043-Votive Candle	Drawn by cvs
044-Sanctuary Light	No results on tineye or google
045-Sword&Book	Drawn by cvs
046-Haircut	https://pixabay.com/vectors/abstinence-ascetic-asceticism-cowl-1296654/
047-Boat	https://publicdomainvectors.org/en/free-clipart/Jesuss-miracles-vector-image/69011.html
048-Keys	Barousse Designs, Picayune, MS
049-Anchor	https://www.wikiwand.com/en/Christian_cross_variants
050-Shell	http://www.gocek.org/christiansymbols/images/escallop.gif
051-Halo	https://publicdomainvectors.org/en/free-clipart/Christmas-nativity-scene/36523.html
052-Lily	https://publicdomainvectors.org/en/free-clipart/Lilies-in-black-and- white/76107.html
053-Fleur de Lis	https://publicdomainvectors.org/en/free-clipart/A-fleur-de-lis-vector-image/8473.html
054-San Damiano	https://commons.wikimedia.org/wiki/File:Kruis_san_damiano.gif#/media/File:Krucifikso_de_Sankta_Damiano.png

055-Swastika	https://www.wikiwand.com/en/Christian_cross_variants
056-Ankh	https://www.wikiwand.com/en/Christian_cross_variants
057-Tau	https://www.wikiwand.com/en/Christian_cross_variants
058-Eastern	https://www.wikiwand.com/en/Christian_cross_variants
059-Jerusalem	https://www.wikiwand.com/en/Christian_cross_variants
060-Latin	https://www.wikiwand.com/en/Christian_cross_variants
061-Greek	https://www.wikiwand.com/en/Christian_cross_variants
062-Maltese	https://www.wikiwand.com/en/Christian_cross_variants
063-St Andrews	https://www.wikiwand.com/en/Christian_cross_variants
064-Celtic	https://publicdomainvectors.org/en/free-clipart/Celtic-cross-in-black-color/77224.html
065-St Brigids	https://www.wikiwand.com/en/Christian_cross_variants
066-Patriarchal	https://www.wikiwand.com/en/Christian_cross_variants
067-Crucifix Skull Crossbones	Drawn by cvs
068-Cross&Jesus	https://www.wikiwand.com/en/Christian_cross_variants
069-Our Lady-blue&snake	Traced from Picture of statue in chapel by cvs
070-Seven Swords	Drawn by cvs
071-Apparitions	https://en.wikipedia.org/wiki/Lourdes_apparitions#/media/File:Notre_Dame_de_Lourdes.JPG
072-Angels	https://publicdomainvectors.org/en/free-clipart/Angel-Gabriel/36612.html
073-Communion of Saints	Drawn by cvs
074-Saints	https://upload.wikimedia.org/wikipedia/commons/5/5a/Saint_Teresa_of_Calcutta.jpg
075-Names	Drawn by cvs
076-Infant of Prague	https://catholicsaints.info/infant-jesus-of-prague/
077-Statue of St Joseph	https://commons.wikimedia.org/wiki/Category:Saint_Joseph#/media/File:Igreja_de_S%C3%A3o_Jo%C3%A3o_de_Brito_9107.jpg
078-St Joseph Altar	Picture of St. Joseph's Altar by a friend
079-St Anthony&Child	Drawn by cvs
080-St Anthony Lost Objects	Drawn by cvs

081-S.A.G.	Drawn by cvs
082-Pope	https://publicdomainvectors.org/en/free-clipart/Vector-drawing-of-the-Pope/4045.html
083-White Cassock	With permission https://catholicsaints.info/cassock/
084-Name Change	Drawn by cvs
085-Conclave	Drawn by cvs
086-Bishop&Crosier	https://publicdomainvectors.org/en/free-clipart/Vector-drawing-of-Christian-bishop/4043.html
087-Ring	https://commons.wikimedia.org/wiki/File:English_-_Bishop%27s_Ring_-_Walters_57481_-_View_A.jpg
088-Zucchetto	https://publicdomainvectors.org/en/free-clipart/Vector-drawing-of-the-Pope/4045.html
089-Biretta	http://www.marysrosaries.com/collaboration/index.php?title=File:Priest_Wearing_a_Biretta_001.jpg
090-Mitre	https://en.wikipedia.org/wiki/Mitre#/media/File:Mitre_evolution.gif
091-Pallium	https://en.wikipedia.org/wiki/Pallium#/media/File:Pallium_(Geschichte).jpg
092-Pectoral Cross	https://publicdomainvectors.org/en/free-clipart/Vector-drawing-of-the-Pope/4045.html
093-Priest	https://publicdomainvectors.org/en/free-clipart/Vector-drawing-of-a-priest/4046.html
094-Priesthood	Drawn by cvs
095-Cassock	With permission https://catholicsaints.info/cassock/
096-Men of The Cloth	https://publicdomainvectors.org/en/free-clipart/Priest-silhouette/66815.html
097-Roman Collar	https://publicdomainvectors.org/en/free-clipart/Vector-drawing-of-a-priest/4046.html
098-Deacon	https://publicdomainvectors.org/en/free-clipart/Vector-drawing-of-Christian-deacon/4044.html
099-Nun	https://pixy.org/650670/
100-Brother&Monk	https://pixabay.com/vectors/abstinence-ascetic-asceticism-cowl-1296654/
101-Hermit	With permission catholicsaints.info/saint-paul-the-hermit/

102-Third Order&Consecrated Life	Drawn by cvs
103-Laity	https://publicdomainvectors.org/en/free-clipart/Going-to-Church/53484.html
104-Liturgy	https://publicdomainvectors.org/en/free-clipart/Illustration-of-church-interior-in-vector-graphics/4034.html
105-Mass	http://www.marysrosaries.com/collaboration/index.php?title=File:Celebrating_Mass.jpg
106-Wheat etc	https://publicdomainvectors.org/en/free-clipart/Bread-and-wine/73028.html
107-Loaves&Fishes	https://publicdomainvectors.org/en/free-clipart/Fish-and-bread/43871.html
108-Bread&Wine	https://publicdomainvectors.org/en/free-clipart/Christian-sacrament/73018.html
109-Kind of Bread	https://publicdomainvectors.org/en/free-clipart/Outline-vector-image-of-bread/30531.html
110-Host	Camera shot of Fr.John's host
111- Holy Communion on Tongue	Drawn by cvs – Using as model https://en.wikipedia.org/wiki/Eucharist_in_the_Catholic_Church#/media/File:Tatiana_Communion2.jpg
112-Language	Written by cvs to emulate the style of each language
113-Raising Host&Chalice	Drawn by cvs
114-Where First Celebrated	Drawn by cvs
115-Obligation	Drawn by cvs
116-Book of Gospels	Camera shot of the Book
117-Roman Missal	https://commons.wikimedia.org/wiki/File:Missale_Romanum.jpg
118-Tridentine Mass	http://www.marysrosaries.com/collaboration/index.php?title=File:Celebrating_Mass.jpg
119-Liturgy of Hours	Camera shot of the Books
120-Adoration	http://www.marysrosaries.com/collaboration/index.php?title=File:Adore2.jpg

121-Eucharistic Congress	https://upload.wikimedia.org/wikipedia/commons/e/ec/41st_Eucharistic_Congress_01_B0992_NLGRF_photo_contact_sheet_%281976-08-08%29%28Gerald_Ford_Library%29.jpg
122-Exposition	Camera shot of Fr. John's Monstrance
123-Benediction	https://en.wikipedia.org/wiki/Eucharistic_adoration#/media/File:Saint_Peter_Julian_Eymard_3rd_class_relic_prayer_card.jpg
124-Blessings	Drawn by cvs
125-Imposition	https://en.wikipedia.org/wiki/File:Holy_Orders_Picture.jpg
126-Sign of the Cross	*Learning to Serve* by Fr. Charles Carmody, St. Augustine Academy Press (first published April 4th 1961) found on Public Domain Books And Joined Hands from https://pixabay.com/vectors/praying-hands-religion-pray-prayer-25596/
127-Prostration	https://en.wikipedia.org/wiki/Prostration#/media/File:Deacon_Ordination.jpg
128-Orans	https://en.wikipedia.org/wiki/Orans#/media/File:Neupivaemaya_Chasha.jpg
129-Joined Hands	https://pixabay.com/vectors/praying-hands-religion-pray-prayer-25596/
130-Genuflection	*Learning to Serve* by Fr. Charles Carmody, St. Augustine Academy Press (first published April 4th 1961) found on Public Domain Books
131-Chalice&Paten	Camera shot of Fr. John's chalice and paten
132-Monstrance	Camera shot of Fr. John's Monstrance
133-Pyx	https://pixy.org/351219/
134-Tabernacle	Camera shot in a chapel
135-Colors	Typed list of Vestmant colors
136-137-Alb&Cincture	https://freesvg.org/alb
138-Stole	Camera shot of Fr. John's Vestment
139-Maniple	Camera shot of Fr. John's Vestment
140-Chasuble	Camera shot of Fr. John's Vestment
141-Cope	http://www.marysrosaries.com/collaboration/index.php?title=File:Cope_001.png

142-Humeral	https://en.wikipedia.org/wiki/Eucharistic_adoration#/media/File:Saint_Peter_Julian_Eymard_3rd_class_relic_prayer_card.jpg
143-Fasting	Drawn by cvs
144-No Meat	Drawn by cvs
145-Fast&Abstain	Drawn by cvs
146-Fish	https://publicdomainvectors.org/en/free-clipart/Blue-fish-vector-clip-art/64315.html
147-CCC	Camera shot of Fr. John's CCC
147-Emblem CCC	https://commons.wikimedia.org/wiki/File:Emblem_of_the_Catechism_of_the_Catholic_Church.jpg
148-First Built	https://en.wikipedia.org/wiki/Early_centers_of_Christianity#/media/File:Antioch_Saint_Pierre_Church_Front.JPG
149-Facing East	Drawn by cvs
150-Steeple	http://www.clker.com/clipart-church-1.html
151-Pews	https://pixy.org/src/57/572440.jpg
152-Chair	Not Found On Google & Tineye
153-Pulpit	https://www.learnersdictionary.com/definition/pulpit
154-Relics	Camera shot of Fr. John's Relics
155-Altar	http://clipart-library.com/clipart/n1058153.htm
156-Icons	https://en.wikipedia.org/wiki/Icon#/media/File:Spas_vsederzhitel_sinay.jpg
157-Holy See	https://en.wikipedia.org/wiki/Pope_Benedict_XVI#/media/File:Pope_Benedict_XVI_1.jpg
158-Statues	Camera shot of statues
159-Sunday	https://publicdomainvectors.org/en/free-clipart/Triquetra-drawing/31952.html
160-Monday	Painting by Bini Roche using as model the prayer card *Summary of Norms for Gaining Indulgences for the Souls in Purgatory or Oneself* (… by Pope Paul VI January 1,1967) With permission from Apostolate for Family Consecration 1-740-567-7700
161-Tuesday	https://publicdomainvectors.org/en/free-clipart/Angel-Gabriel/36612.html
162-Wednesday	http://marysrosaries.com/collaboration/index.php?title=File:St_Joseph_with_Child_Jesus_001.jpg

163-Thursday	https://publicdomainvectors.org/en/free-clipart/The-Blessed-Sacrament-vector-image/6458.html
164-Friday	Embroidery by unknown
165-Saturday	https://publicdomainvectors.org/en/free-clipart/Virgin-Mary-vector-drawing/6434.html
166-January	https://publicdomainvectors.org/en/free-clipart/Virgin-Mary-and-baby-Jesus/74060.html
167-February	https://publicdomainvectors.org/en/free-clipart/Interpretation-of-the-nativity-scene/36522.html
168-March	http://marysrosaries.com/collaboration/index.php?title=File:St_Joseph_with_Child_Jesus_001.jpg
169-April	Drawn by cvs
170-May	https://upload.wikimedia.org/wikipedia/commons/2/2c/Virgen_de_guadalupe1.jpg
171-June	https://en.wikipedia.org/wiki/Sacred_Heart#/media/File:Sagrado_Cora%C3%A7%C3%A3o_de_Jesus_-_escola_portuguesa,_s%C3%A9culo_XIX.png
172-July	Embroidery by unknown
173-August	https://publicdomainvectors.org/en/free-clipart/The-Blessed-Sacrament-vector-image/6458.html
174-September	Drawn by cvs
175-October	http://www.clker.com/clipart-630993.html
176-November	Painting by Bini Roche using as model the prayer card *Summary of Norms for Gaining Indulgences for the Souls in Purgatory or Oneself* (… by Pope Paul VI January 1,1967) With permission from Apostolate for Family Consecration 1-740-567-7700
177-December	https://en.wikipedia.org/wiki/Lourdes_apparitions#/media/File:Notre_Dame_de_Lourdes.JPG
178-Gregorian Calendar	https://en.wikipedia.org/wiki/Conversion_between_Julian_and_Gregorian_calendars#/media/File:Julian_to_Gregorian_Date_Change.png
179-Jubilee Year	https://en.wikipedia.org/wiki/Jubilee_in_the_Catholic_Church#/media/File:Heilig_jaar_souvenir.jpg
180-Our Father	https://www.wpclipart.com/religion_mythology/new_testament/Jesus/sermon_on_the_mount_BW.png.html
181-Hail Mary	https://pixy.org/749983/

182-Rosary	http://www.clker.com/clipart-630993.html
183-Angelus	https://publicdomainvectors.org/en/free-clipart/Old-bell-vector-image/2786.html
184-Litany	Typed
185-Stations	http://www.clker.com/clipart-721138.html
186-Pilgrimage	https://webcomicms.net/ clipart-9736565-pilgrimage-cliparts
187-Novena	http://webcomicms.net/clipart-10044479-pentecost-pics
188-OLOG	https://upload.wikimedia.org/wikipedia/commons/2/2c/ Virgen_de_guadalupe1.jpg
188-Tilma & 192-Flowers	https://media.ascensionpress.com/ https://media.ascensionpress.com/2018/12/12/ juan-diego-changed-new-world/ used with permission
189-191 & 193-203	Scan of tapestries of Our Lady of Guadalupe owned by cvs

Made in the USA
Coppell, TX
15 February 2026

72097632R00090